The Standard for English Grammar Books

GRAMMAR ZONE
WORKBOOK

기본편 2

GRAMMAR ZONE WORKBOOK 기본편 2

지은이	NE능률 영어교육연구소
선임연구원	한정은
연구원	배연희 이하나 송민아 이경란 강혜진
영문교열	Patrick Ferraro Benjamin Robinson
표지 · 내지디자인	닷츠
내지일러스트	김나나
맥편집	허문희
영업	한기영 이경구 박인규 정철교 김남준 이우현
마케팅	박혜선 남경진 이지원 김여진

43 SINCE 1980 rd
Let's grow together
NE능률이
미래를
창조합니다.
건강한 배움의 고객가치를 제공하겠다는 꿈을 실현하기 위해
40년이 넘는 시간 동안 열심히 달려왔습니다.
앞으로도 끊임없는 연구와 노력을 통해
당연한 것을 멈추지 않고
고객, 기업, 직원 모두가 함께 성장하는 NE능률이 되겠습니다.
NE 능률

Practice is the best of all instructions.

연습은 가장 좋은 가르침이다.

유명한 운동 선수, 최고의 과학자, 노벨상을 받은 작가, 그 누구도 자신들이 이루어낸 것이 하루 아침에 완성되었다고 말하는 사람은 없습니다. 그들을 성공으로 이끈 것은 무엇일까요? 여러분도 알다시피 목표를 달성하고 꿈을 이루는 데 성실하게 연습하는 것만큼 효과적인 무기는 없습니다. 저희는 여러분을 '문법 지존(至尊)'의 세계로 인도할 수 있는 가장 좋은 무기를 준비하였습니다. G-ZONE에서 학습한 모든 것을 이 WORKBOOK을 통해 연습하여 여러분 모두 문법의 '지존'이 되길 바랍니다. 꾸준한 연습을 다짐하는 여러분을 응원합니다.

구성과 특징

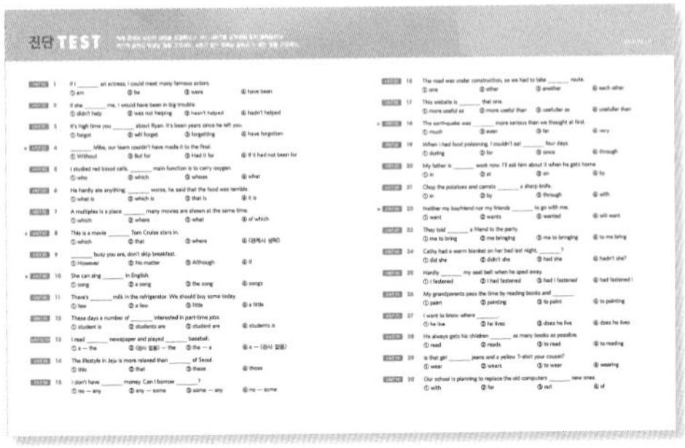

진단 TEST

현재 자신이 알고 있는 문법 항목과 모르는 문법 항목을 점검할 수 있게 하는 TEST입니다. WORKBOOK을 본격적으로 공부하기 전에 진단 TEST부터 풀어 보고, 자신이 부족한 부분이 어디인지 파악한 후 학습 계획을 세워 봅시다. 각 문제 옆에는 연관된 Grammar Zone 본 교재의 UNIT이 표기되어 있으니, 틀린 문제에 해당하는 UNIT을 본 교재로 먼저 복습하면 효율적인 학습이 가능합니다.

TEST

각 UNIT을 제대로 학습하였는지 확인할 수 있는 다양한 유형의 문제를 수록하였습니다. 비교적 간단한 드릴형 문제에서부터 사고력과 응용력을 요하는 문제까지 꼼꼼히 풀어본 후 부족한 부분에 대해 추가 학습 계획을 세워 봅시다.

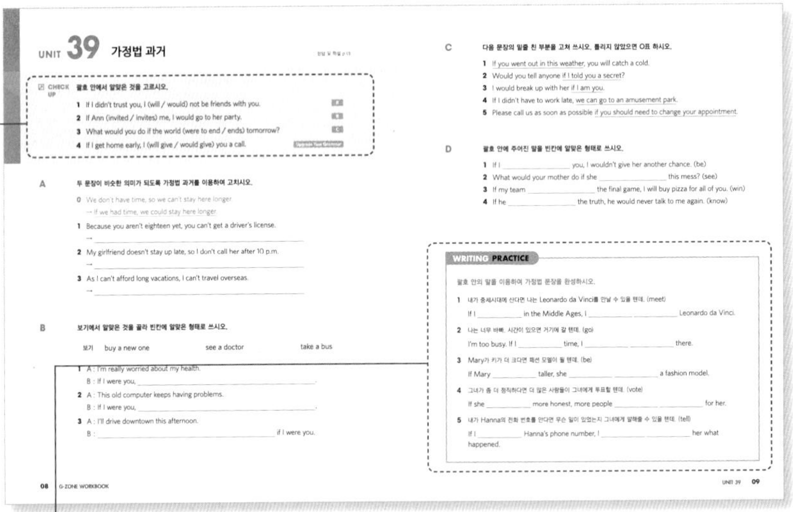

UNIT 39 가정법 과거

CHECK UP 괄호 안에서 알맞은 것을 고르시오.

1 If I didn't trust you, I (will / would) not be friends with you.
2 If Ann (invited / invites) me, I would go to her party.
3 What would you do if the world (were to end / ends) tomorrow?
4 If I get home early, I (will give / would give) you a call.

A 두 문장이 비슷한 의미가 되도록 가정법 과거를 이용하여 고치시오.

0 We don't have time, so we can't stay here longer.
→ If we had time, we could stay here longer.
1 Because you aren't eighteen yet, you can't get a driver's license.
→
2 My girlfriend doesn't stay up late, so I don't call her after 10 p.m.
→
3 As I can't afford long vacations, I can't travel overseas.
→

B 보기에서 알맞은 것을 골라 빈칸에 알맞은 형태로 쓰시오.

보기 buy a new one / see a doctor / take a bus

1 A : I'm really worried about my health.
B : If I were you, ______.
2 A : This old computer keeps having problems.
B : If I were you, ______.
3 A : I'll drive downtown this afternoon.
B : ______ if I were you.

08 G-ZONE WORKBOOK

C 다음 문장의 밑줄 친 부분을 고쳐 쓰시오. 틀리지 않았으면 O표 하시오.

1 If you went out in this weather, you will catch a cold.
2 Would you tell anyone if I told you a secret?
3 I would break up with her if I am you.
4 If I didn't have to work late, we can go to an amusement park.
5 Please call us as soon as possible if you should need to change your appointment.

D 괄호 안에 주어진 말을 빈칸에 알맞은 형태로 쓰시오.

1 If I ______ you, I wouldn't give her another chance. (be)
2 What would your mother do if she ______ this mess? (see)
3 If my team ______ the final game, I will buy pizza for all of you. (win)
4 If he ______ the truth, he would never talk to me again. (know)

WRITING PRACTICE

괄호 안의 말을 이용하여 가정법 문장을 완성하시오.

1 내가 중세시대에 산다면 나는 Leonardo da Vinci를 만날 수 있을 텐데. (meet)
If I ______ in the Middle Ages, I ______ ______ Leonardo da Vinci.
2 나는 너무 바빠. 시간이 있으면 거기에 갈 텐데. (go)
I'm too busy. If I ______ time, I ______ ______ there.
3 Mary가 키가 더 크다면 패션 모델이 될 텐데. (be)
If Mary ______ taller, she ______ ______ a fashion model.
4 그녀가 좀 더 정직하다면 더 많은 사람들이 그녀에게 투표할 텐데. (vote)
If she ______ more honest, more people ______ ______ for her.
5 내가 Hanna의 전화 번호를 안다면 무슨 일이 있었는지 그녀에게 말해줄 수 있을 텐데. (tell)
If I ______ Hanna's phone number, I ______ ______ her what happened.

UNIT 39 09

CHECK UP

각 UNIT의 핵심 문법을 간단한 문제를 통해 확인할 수 있습니다. 각 문제 옆에는 해당 문법을 다룬 본 교재의 항목이 표시되어 있으므로, 추가 학습이 필요하다면 해당 항목을 복습한 후 WORKBOOK으로 돌아오세요.

WRITING PRACTICE

쓰기 연습이 가능한 문제를 충분히 제시하였습니다. 수행평가나 서술형 문제 대비가 가능하며 궁극적으로 영어 쓰기 실력을 향상시켜 줍니다.

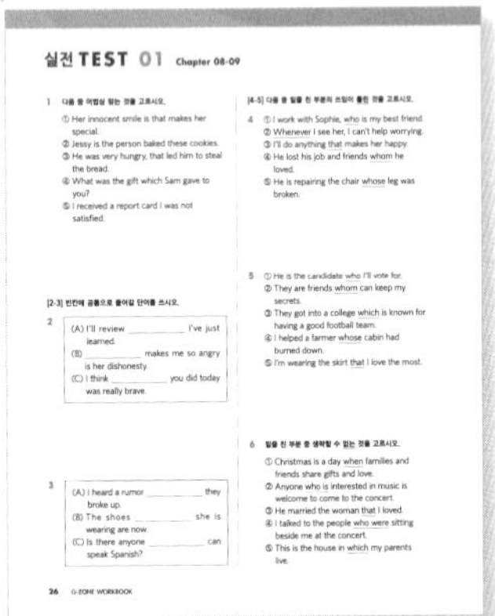

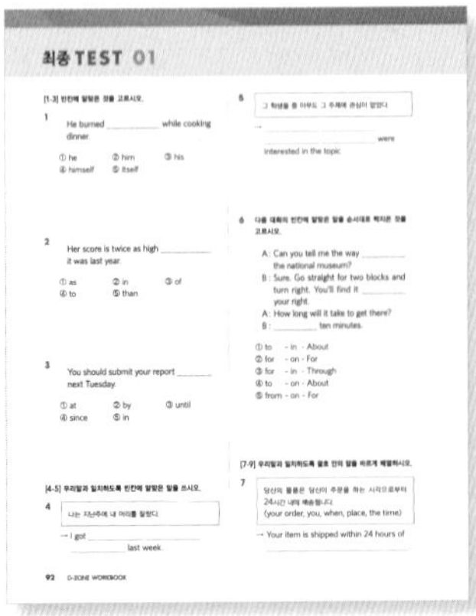

실전 TEST & 최종 TEST

여러 CHAPTER의 문법 사항을 종합적으로 확인할 수 있도록 총 6회의 실전 TEST와 4회의 최종 TEST를 제공합니다. 중간고사 및 기말고사에 대비할 수 있도록 문제 유형과 난이도 등을 실제에 맞추어 구성하였으며, 실제 기출을 응용한 주관식 문제를 제시하여 수행평가 및 서술형 문제 대비에도 유용합니다.

Contents

Study Tracker

그래머존 본책의 학습일을 기입한 후, 워크북으로 확인 학습한 날짜도 함께 적어 봅시다. 워크북까지 학습을 끝낸 후 '나의 문법 이해도'를 점검해 봅시다.

본책 CHAPTER / 학습일	워크북 TEST / 학습일	나의 문법 이해도
	진단 TEST 월 일	상 중 하
CHAPTER 08 가정법 월 일	39 월 일 40 월 일 41 월 일 42 월 일	상 중 하
CHAPTER 09 관계사 월 일	43 월 일 44 월 일 45 월 일 46 월 일 47 월 일	상 중 하
	실전 TEST 01 월 일	상 중 하
CHAPTER 10 명사와 관사 월 일	48 월 일 49 월 일 50 월 일 51 월 일	상 중 하
CHAPTER 11 대명사 월 일	52 월 일 53 월 일 54 월 일 55 월 일	상 중 하
CHAPTER 12 형용사와 부사, 비교 월 일	56 월 일 57 월 일 58 월 일 59 월 일	상 중 하
	실전 TEST 02 월 일	상 중 하
CHAPTER 13 전치사 월 일	60 월 일 61 월 일 62 월 일 63 월 일 64 월 일 65 월 일	상 중 하
CHAPTER 14 일치 및 화법, 특수구문 월 일	66 월 일 67 월 일 68 월 일 69 월 일 70 월 일	상 중 하
CHAPTER 15 독해력 향상을 위한 문장구조 이해하기 월 일	71 월 일 72 월 일 73 월 일 74 월 일	상 중 하
	실전 TEST 03 월 일	상 중 하
	최종 TEST 01 월 일	상 중 하
	최종 TEST 02 월 일	상 중 하

진단 TEST

아래 문제로 자신의 실력을 점검해보고, 어느 UNIT을 공부해야 할지 알아봅시다.
빈칸에 들어갈 알맞은 말을 고르세요. ★표가 있는 문제는 들어갈 수 없는 말을 고르세요.

UNIT 39 **1** If I ________ an actress, I could meet many famous actors.
① am ② be ③ were ④ have been

UNIT 40 **2** If she ________ me, I would have been in big trouble.
① didn't help ② was not helping ③ hasn't helped ④ hadn't helped

UNIT 41 **3** It's high time you ________ about Ryan. It's been years since he left you.
① forgot ② will forget ③ forgetting ④ have forgotten

★ UNIT 42 **4** ________ Mike, our team couldn't have made it to the final.
① Without ② But for ③ Had it for ④ If it had not been for

UNIT 43, 46 **5** I studied red blood cells, ________ main function is to carry oxygen.
① who ② which ③ whose ④ what

UNIT 44 **6** He hardly ate anything; ________ worse, he said that the food was terrible.
① what is ② which is ③ that is ④ it is

UNIT 45 **7** A multiplex is a place ________ many movies are shown at the same time.
① which ② where ③ what ④ of which

★ UNIT 47 **8** This is a movie ________ Tom Cruise stars in.
① which ② that ③ where ④ (관계사 생략)

UNIT 47 **9** ________ busy you are, don't skip breakfast.
① However ② No matter ③ Although ④ If

★ UNIT 48 **10** She can sing ________ in English.
① song ② a song ③ the song ④ songs

UNIT 49 **11** There's ________ milk in the refrigerator. We should buy some today.
① few ② a few ③ little ④ a little

UNIT 49 **12** These days a number of ________ interested in part-time jobs.
① student is ② students are ③ student are ④ students is

UNIT 50, 51 **13** I read ________ newspaper and played ________ baseball.
① a — the ② (관사 없음) — the ③ the — a ④ a — (관사 없음)

UNIT 53 **14** The lifestyle in Jeju is more relaxed than ________ of Seoul.
① this ② that ③ these ④ those

UNIT 54 **15** I don't have ________ money. Can I borrow ________?
① no — any ② any — some ③ some — any ④ no — some

정답 및 해설 p.02

UNIT 55 **16** The road was under construction, so we had to take ________ route.
① one ② other ③ another ④ each other

UNIT 58 **17** This website is ________ that one.
① more useful as ② more useful than ③ usefuller as ④ usefuller than

★ UNIT 58 **18** The earthquake was ________ more serious than we thought at first.
① much ② even ③ far ④ very

UNIT 61 **19** When I had food poisoning, I couldn't eat ________ four days.
① during ② for ③ since ④ through

UNIT 63 **20** My father is ________ work now. I'll ask him about it when he gets home.
① in ② at ③ on ④ by

UNIT 64 **21** Chop the potatoes and carrots ________ a sharp knife.
① in ② by ③ through ④ with

★ UNIT 66 **22** Neither my boyfriend nor my friends ________ to go with me.
① want ② wants ③ wanted ④ will want

UNIT 67 **23** They told ________ a friend to the party.
① me to bring ② me bringing ③ me to bringing ④ to me bring

UNIT 68 **24** Cathy had a warm blanket on her bed last night, ________?
① did she ② didn't she ③ had she ④ hadn't she?

UNIT 69 **25** Hardly ________ my seat belt when he sped away.
① I fastened ② I had fastened ③ had I fastened ④ had fastened I

UNIT 70 **26** My grandparents pass the time by reading books and ________.
① paint ② painting ③ to paint ④ to painting

UNIT 71 **27** I want to know where ________.
① he live ② he lives ③ does he live ④ does he lives

UNIT 72 **28** He always gets his children ________ as many books as possible.
① read ② reads ③ to read ④ to reading

UNIT 73 **29** Is that girl ________ jeans and a yellow T-shirt your cousin?
① wear ② wears ③ to wear ④ wearing

UNIT 74 **30** Our school is planning to replace the old computers ________ new ones.
① with ② for ③ out ④ of

UNIT 39 가정법 과거

정답 및 해설 p.03

CHECK UP 괄호 안에서 알맞은 것을 고르시오.

1 If I didn't trust you, I (will / would) not be friends with you. B

2 If Ann (invited / invites) me, I would go to her party. B

3 What would you do if the world (were to end / ends) tomorrow? C

4 If I get home early, I (will give / would give) you a call. Upgrade Your Grammar

A 두 문장이 비슷한 의미가 되도록 가정법 과거를 이용하여 고치시오.

0 We don't have time, so we can't stay here longer.
→ If we had time, we could stay here longer.

1 Because you aren't eighteen yet, you can't get a driver's license.
→ ______________________________

2 My girlfriend doesn't stay up late, so I don't call her after 10 p.m.
→ ______________________________

3 As I can't afford long vacations, I can't travel overseas.
→ ______________________________

B 보기에서 알맞은 것을 골라 빈칸에 알맞은 형태로 쓰시오.

보기 buy a new one / see a doctor / take a bus

1 A : I'm really worried about my health.
B : If I were you, ______________________________.

2 A : This old computer keeps having problems.
B : If I were you, ______________________________.

3 A : I'll drive downtown this afternoon.
B : ______________________________ if I were you.

C 다음 문장의 밑줄 친 부분을 고쳐 쓰시오. 틀리지 않았으면 O표 하시오.

1 If you went out in this weather, you will catch a cold.
2 Would you tell anyone if I told you a secret?
3 I would break up with her if I am you.
4 If I didn't have to work late, we can go to an amusement park.
5 Please call us as soon as possible if you should need to change your appointment.

D 괄호 안에 주어진 말을 빈칸에 알맞은 형태로 쓰시오.

1 If I ______ you, I wouldn't give her another chance. (be)
2 What would your mother do if she ______ this mess? (see)
3 If my team ______ the final game, I will buy pizza for all of you. (win)
4 If he ______ the truth, he would never talk to me again. (know)

WRITING PRACTICE

괄호 안의 말을 이용하여 가정법 문장을 완성하시오.

1 내가 중세시대에 산다면 나는 Leonardo da Vinci를 만날 수 있을 텐데. (meet)

If I ______ in the Middle Ages, I ______ ______ Leonardo da Vinci.

2 나는 너무 바빠. 시간이 있으면 거기에 갈 텐데. (go)

I'm too busy. If I ______ time, I ______ ______ there.

3 Mary가 키가 더 크다면 패션 모델이 될 텐데. (be)

If Mary ______ taller, she ______ ______ a fashion model.

4 그녀가 좀 더 정직하다면 더 많은 사람들이 그녀에게 투표할 텐데. (vote)

If she ______ more honest, more people ______ ______ for her.

5 내가 Hanna의 전화 번호를 안다면 무슨 일이 있었는지 그녀에게 말해줄 수 있을 텐데. (tell)

If I ______ Hanna's phone number, I ______ ______ her what happened.

UNIT 40 가정법 과거완료, 혼합 가정법

정답 및 해설 p.04

CHECK UP 괄호 안에서 알맞은 것을 고르시오.

1 If we (have known / had known) that you were coming, we would have waited for you. B

2 If I (checked / had checked) my bag earlier, I would have noticed that I left my purse at home. B

3 I (will / would) have invited you to the movies if I had known you like comedies. B

4 You wouldn't (be / have been) sick now if you had dressed warmer. C

A

다음 문장을 보기와 같이 가정법 과거완료나 혼합 가정법을 이용하여 고치시오.

0 I didn't know that it was Emily's birthday, so I didn't buy her a gift.
→ If I had known that it was Emily's birthday, I would have bought her a gift.

1 Because all the tickets were sold out, I couldn't watch the baseball game at the stadium.
→ If ____.

2 Because everyone was talking so loudly, we couldn't hear the announcement.
→ If ____.

3 Because nobody helped me, I am in trouble now.
→ If ____.

B

보기에서 알맞은 것을 골라 빈칸에 알맞은 형태로 쓰시오.

보기 be scolded / open the door for her / join you for dinner now / finish your report

1 If I had heard the doorbell ring, ________________________.

2 If you hadn't been so lazy, ________________________.

3 If I had not eaten already, ________________________.

4 If Tom had cleaned his room, ________________________ by his mother.

C 다음 문장의 밑줄 친 부분을 고쳐 쓰시오. 틀리지 않았으면 O표 하시오.

1 If I have studied harder, I would have passed the history test.
2 If someone had called the police, the thief would have been caught.
3 You might not have been rich now if you had not listened to my advice.
4 We could have prevented the accident if we had been more careful.
5 I wouldn't have spent a night at the airport if I didn't miss my flight.

D 괄호 안의 말을 이용하여 대화를 완성하시오.

1 A : I heard you almost had an accident last week.
B : Yes, the car in front of me stopped suddenly. If I ______________ on the brakes, I would have crashed. (slam)

2 A : Harry, did you go to the dentist in the morning?
B : Oh, I completely forgot. If you had reminded me, I ______________ the appointment. (forget)

WRITING PRACTICE

보기에 주어진 말을 이용하여 가정법 과거완료나 혼합 가정법 문장을 완성하시오.

보기 ask meet own visit

1 시간이 충분히 있었다면 너를 방문했을 텐데.
If I ________ enough time, I ______________ you.

2 내가 너를 봤다면 너희 가족에 관해 물어볼 수 있었을 텐데.
If I ________ you, I ______________ you about your family.

3 내가 돈을 저축했다면 지금 차를 갖고 있을 텐데.
If I ________ money, I ______________ a car now.

4 네가 온다는 걸 알았더라면 나는 역에서 너를 만났을 텐데.
If I ________ you were coming, I ______________ at the station.

UNIT 41 I wish / as if [though] / It's time + 가정법

정답 및 해설 p.06

CHECK UP 괄호 안에서 알맞은 것을 고르시오.

1 I wish Jessica (is / were) my sister. A-1

2 I wish I (had / had had) this book earlier so I could have studied it for my exam. A-2

3 He is not an expert, but he talks as if he (is / were) one. B-1

4 It's time she (will pack / packed) her bag. She needs to leave in an hour. C

A

괄호 안에 주어진 문장을 「I wish + 가정법」 문장으로 고치시오.

1 (I'm sorry that you didn't get the job you applied for.)
→ I wish ______________________________.

2 (I'm sorry that I can't go to her concert this weekend.)
→ I wish ______________________________.

3 (I'm sorry that my father doesn't understand me.)
→ I wish ______________________________.

4 (I'm sorry that my brother isn't here with us.)
→ I wish ______________________________.

5 (I'm sorry that I didn't watch the soccer match on TV last night.)
→ I wish ______________________________.

B

괄호 안의 문장과 의미가 통하도록 빈칸에 알맞은 말을 쓰시오.

0 He talks as if he knew everything. (In fact, he doesn't know everything.)

1 Sometimes you act as if ______________________. (In fact, you aren't a little girl.)

2 She spends money as if ______________________. (In fact, she isn't rich.)

3 He acted as if ______________________. (In fact, he had witnessed the accident.)

4 She wept as if ______________________. (In fact, she hadn't lost her own son.)

5 She was talking as if ______________________. (In fact, she hasn't lived in Paris.)

C 괄호 안에 주어진 말을 빈칸에 알맞은 형태로 쓰시오.

1 It's high time he ________________ getting dressed. He has to leave for the party soon. (begin)

2 We had a big fight, but later she acted as if nothing ________________. (happen)

3 Now I'm broke. I wish I ________________ all my money so quickly. (not, spend)

4 My son always skips breakfast. I wish he ________________ breakfast. (eat)

5 Nicole didn't attend the meeting. I wish she ________________. (come)

D 다음 문장에서 어법상 틀린 곳을 찾아 고치시오. 틀린 곳이 없으면 O표 하시오.

1 The lake we went to was really beautiful. I wish you have seen it.

2 It is time you started showing some appreciation to others.

3 I wish I had more money to buy a new computer.

4 He talked as if he made the soup, but actually his sister made it.

WRITING PRACTICE

괄호 안의 말을 이용하여 가정법 문장을 완성하시오.

1 거기에 가는 방법을 안다면 좋을 텐데. (how, to get)

I wish I ____________ ____________ ____________ ____________ there.

2 그는 자신이 마치 중국에 가 본 것처럼 말했다. (be)

He talked ____________ ____________ he ____________ ____________ to China.

3 Serena는 마치 며칠 동안 잠을 자지 못했던 것처럼 자고 있다. (sleep)

Serena is sleeping ____________ ____________ she ____________ ____________ ____________ for days.

4 그녀의 생일이었다고 그녀가 말해줬더라면 좋았을 텐데. (wish, tell)

I ____________ ____________ ____________ ____________ us it was her birthday.

5 참 지저분하네! 이제 정말 우리가 이 창고를 깨끗이 정리할 때야. (about, clean out)

What a mess! It's ____________ time we ____________ ____________ this shed!

UNIT 42 주의해야 할 가정법

정답 및 해설 p.07

CHECK UP 괄호 안에서 알맞은 것을 고르시오.

1 (Should you / You should) have any questions, feel free to ask me. B

2 It would be shocking (see a real dragon / to see a real dragon). C

3 (Without / But) for his early death, he would have become king. A

4 (It were not for / Were it not for) the rain, we would go out for a walk. B

A 주어진 문장과 같은 뜻이 되도록 빈칸을 채우시오.

1 To see her house, you would think she was an interior designer.
= If ______________________________.

2 But for the new machine, we couldn't have made the products on time.
= If ______________________________.

3 With your help, he could have won the case.
= If ______________________________.

4 Without laws, our society would be in disorder.
= If ______________________________.

B 다음 문장을 If를 생략하여 같은 뜻이 되도록 고치시오.

1 If you had told me you were coming, I would have prepared a room for you.
= ______________________________

2 If I were you, I would hire him as my secretary.
= ______________________________

3 If I had known his real intention, I would not have supported him.
= ______________________________

C

다음 문장의 밑줄 친 부분을 고쳐 쓰시오. 틀리지 않았으면 O표 하시오.

1 An American would not pronounce the word that way.

2 We could get lost but she gave us quite clear directions.

3 Without the stock market crash, the company wouldn't have gone bankrupt.

4 Were we earlier, we could have caught the last train to Busan.

5 If it were not for the brave firefighters, many people could have been hurt.

D

괄호 안에 주어진 말과 가정법을 이용하여 빈칸을 완성하시오.

1 I had to run; otherwise I ____________ ____________ ____________ the school bus this morning. (miss)

2 ____________ I ____________ about the truth, I would not have trusted her. (know)

3 ____________ it ____________ ____________ email, it would be difficult for us to keep in touch. (not, be)

WRITING PRACTICE

괄호 안의 말을 이용하여 영작을 완성하시오.

1 그의 후원이 없었다면 나는 대학에 갈 수 없었을 것이다. (go)

____________ his support, I ____________ ____________ ____________ ____________ to university.

2 내가 너라면 그의 충고를 받아들일 텐데. (take)

____________ I you, I ____________ ____________ his advice.

3 내가 어제 파티에 갔더라면 Tom을 만날 수 있었을 텐데. (go, meet)

____________ I ____________ to the party yesterday, I ____________ ____________ ____________ Tom.

4 서비스가 더 좋으면 그 식당은 더 많은 손님을 끌어모을 텐데. (draw)

____________ better service, the restaurant ____________ ____________ more customers.

5 도움이 필요하시면, 제가 옆방에 있겠습니다. (should, need)

____________ you ____________ ____________, I will be in the room next door.

UNIT 43 관계대명사 who, whom, whose, which

정답 및 해설 p.09

CHECK UP 괄호 안에서 알맞은 것을 고르시오.

1 In my class there are several boys (who / which) make trouble all the time. B-1

2 Isn't that the man (whom / whose) last name is Williams? B-3

3 I ate lunch with a friend (whom / whose) I hadn't seen in months. B-2

4 We went to the museum (of which / which) reopened after renovations. C-1

A

주어진 두 문장을 관계대명사를 이용하여 한 문장으로 만드시오. (관계대명사 that은 제외)

1 Let's go to the restaurant. It serves dumplings.

→ ______________________________

2 I complained to the man. His dog dug a hole in our front yard.

→ ______________________________

3 I haven't met the people. They moved in next door.

→ ______________________________

4 The software doesn't work well. I downloaded it yesterday.

→ ______________________________

5 These pills are only for patients. Their hearts are unhealthy.

→ ______________________________

B

보기에서 알맞은 관계대명사를 골라 빈칸에 쓰시오. (단, 한 번씩만 쓸 것)

보기 whose who whom which

1 The old lady ______________ lives next door keeps three cats.

2 I know a girl ______________ father works in the White House.

3 The black dress ______________ you bought yesterday suits you well.

4 The people ______________ I spoke to this morning were very helpful.

C

다음 문장의 밑줄 친 부분을 고쳐 쓰시오. 틀리지 않았으면 O표 하시오.

1 She has a rash the cause of which is unknown.
2 I met a guy whom brother is a professional tennis player.
3 I have some friends who they are interested in animal rights.
4 She is the actress which played a space traveler in her last movie.

D

보기에 주어진 말과 관계대명사를 이용하여 문장을 완성하시오. (관계대명사 that은 제외)

보기		
	it features my favorite singers	they were lying on the table
	he served our table	he misses his fiancée during the war

1 We gave a tip to the waiter ______________________________.
2 I created a music blog ______________________________.
3 This poem is about a soldier ______________________________.
4 Where are the car keys ______________________________?

WRITING PRACTICE

괄호 안의 말을 알맞게 배열하여 영작을 완성하시오.

1 나는 네가 쓴 글이 마음에 들었어. (the composition, wrote, you, liked, which)

→ I ______________________________.

2 차를 도난당한 그 여자는 경찰을 불렀다. (was stolen, whose, called, the police, car)

→ The woman ______________________________.

3 Rosa는 그녀가 함께 사는 그녀의 사촌들을 좋아한다. (whom, likes, is, her cousins, living with, she)

→ Rosa ______________________________.

4 내 옆에 앉아 있던 남자는 영화 보는 내내 잠만 잤다. (next to, who, was sitting, me, through the movie, slept)

→ The man ______________________________.

UNIT 44 관계대명사 that, what, 관계대명사의 생략

정답 및 해설 p.10

CHECK UP 괄호 안에서 알맞은 것을 고르시오.

1 (That / What) he told us was a lie. B-1

2 The movie (that / what) we went to was quite boring. A-1

3 I managed to get all the books (that / what) he asked for. A-2

4 The gun (was used / used) in the murder has just been found. C-2

A 빈칸에 관계대명사 that 또는 what 중 알맞은 것을 쓰시오.

1 I told her everything ____________ she wanted to know.

2 Erin is upset because her kids never do ____________ she asks.

3 It's not a good idea to give children everything ____________ they want.

4 I am sorry for ____________ I said. Will you forgive me?

5 Don't buy things if they aren't ____________ you really want.

B 다음 문장에서 생략할 수 있는 부분이 있다면 (   ) 표시 하시오.

1 Where is the CD that I was listening to?

2 The thief who stole my wallet was arrested by the police.

3 I'm working for a man whom I've known for around a decade.

4 There are some students who are waiting outside of the room.

5 What do you think of the movie that we saw yesterday?

6 Do you think we can trust what we find on the Internet?

7 Thomas only drinks juice that is made from organic fruit.

C

다음 문장에서 어법상 틀린 곳을 찾아 고치시오. 틀린 곳이 없으면 O표 하시오.

1 Wisdom is something what comes from experience.
2 Hummingbirds are the only birds can fly backwards.
3 Mr. White is going to tell you what you have to do.
4 The gift I got for my birthday was just that I wanted.
5 Could you hand me the book is sitting on the chair?

D

보기에서 알맞은 것을 모두 골라 빈칸에 쓰시오.

보기	what	whom	who	which	that	✓(생략 가능한 경우)

1 ______________ you need is a good meal and some sleep.
2 The things ______________ he did made us all laugh.
3 An aspirin is ______________ helps me most when I have a headache.
4 The joke ______________ went around the classroom wasn't funny at all.
5 I chatted online with a girl ______________ I had gone to school with.

WRITING PRACTICE

괄호 안의 말을 이용하여 영작을 완성하시오.

1 나는 그녀가 하는 어떤 말도 믿을 수 없다. (anything, say)
I can't believe ________ ________ ________ ________.

2 Steve는 다이어트 중이어서 그가 원하는 것을 먹을 수 없다. (what, want)
Steve is on a diet, so he can't ________ ________ ________ ________.

3 Julie는 예전의 그녀가 아니다. (used to)
Julie is not ________ ________ ________ ________ ________.

4 내게 손을 흔들고 있는 저 여자아이는 내 여동생이다. (wave at)
The girl ________ ________ ________ is my sister.

UNIT 45 관계부사 when, where, why, how

정답 및 해설 p.11

CHECK UP 괄호 안에서 알맞은 것을 고르시오.

1 I'd like to show you the place (where / when) I grew up. B

2 The reason (why / how) the baby cried was that she was hungry. B

3 I remember the day (where / when) my grandmother died. B

4 Show me (the way / the way how) you fixed the camera. B

A 보기에서 알맞은 것을 골라 빈칸에 쓰시오.

보기 the place the reason the time the way

1 ________________ we visited Greece was one of my favorite vacations.

2 Look at ________________ she looks at him.

3 This restaurant is ________________ I like to eat most.

4 Mr. Smith was a heavy smoker. This was probably ________________ he died of lung cancer.

B 주어진 두 문장을 관계부사를 이용하여 한 문장으로 만드시오.

1 Mary's brother found the place. She hid her diary there.
→ Mary's brother found the place ________________________________.

2 Tell me the reason. You never call me anymore for the reason.
→ Tell me the reason ________________________________.

3 Tell me the way. You fixed my broken computer in the way.
→ Tell me ________________________________.

4 July is the month. I see my grandparents the most during the month.
→ July is the month ________________________________.

C 다음 문장의 밑줄 친 부분을 고쳐 쓰시오. 틀리지 않았으면 O표 하시오.

1 This is the place which I call home.
2 I don't know the reason how she is so angry at me.
3 I really can't guess the way how he does those magic tricks.
4 Autumn is when all the leaves change colors.

D 괄호 안의 말을 알맞게 배열하여 문장을 완성하시오.

1 That is (play, the park, used to, we, where) as children.
2 Late at night is (the only, relax, my wife, can, time).
3 Could you tell me (quickly, you, the way, English, learned, so)?
4 (the apartment, she, lives, where) is on the 39th floor.
5 That's (I, the fountain, met, at which) her.

WRITING PRACTICE

괄호 안의 말을 이용하여 영작을 완성하시오.

1 그는 감기에 걸렸다. 그게 바로 그가 그 파티에 오지 못한 이유이다. (why, come)

He caught a cold. That was ________ ________ ________ ________ to the party.

2 그것이 내가 그 문제를 푼 방법이다. (way, solve)

That's ________ ________ I ________ ________ ________.

3 여름은 모두가 해변으로 향하는 계절이다. (season, head)

Summer is ________ ________ ________ everybody ________ to the beach.

4 그가 자라난 그 마을은 매우 작은 곳이다. (town, grow up)

________ ________ ________ he ________ ________ is very small.

UNIT 46 관계사의 계속적 용법

정답 및 해설 p.13

CHECK UP 괄호 안에서 알맞은 것을 고르시오.

1 One of my best friends is Peter, and he lives next door. B-1
= One of my best friends is Peter (who / , who) lives next door.

2 My son works as a translator, and he speaks three languages. B-1
= My son, (who / that) speaks three languages, works as a translator.

3 Mia has just come back from Japan, and she was studying there. B-2
= Mia has just come back from Japan (where / , where) she was studying.

A

의미가 통하는 문장을 연결하고, 관계사의 계속적 용법을 이용하여 한 문장으로 쓰시오.

0 India gained its independence in 1947. •	• a. This makes it hard for me to sleep.
1 I'm going back to Busan. •	• b. His parents are on a business trip.
2 Our train has been delayed. •	• c. It was once a colony of the British.
3 The people upstairs often make noise at night. •	• d. Most of my family and friends live there.
4 I have to take care of my nephew. •	• e. She had an accident about a week ago.
5 Sarah is in the hospital now. •	• f. This means we have to wait an hour.
6 My father teaches physics. •	• g. I want to study it in university.

0 India, which was once a colony of the British, gained its independence in 1947.

1 ______________________________

2 ______________________________

3 ______________________________

4 ______________________________

5 ______________________________

6 ______________________________

B **다음 문장에서 어법상 <u>틀린</u> 곳을 찾아 고치시오. 틀린 곳이 없으면 O표 하시오.**

1 Tom showed me his new tablet, that he uses all the time.

2 Matthew offered to loan me money which was very kind.

3 She sang the Beatles' *Hey Jude*, which I like best.

4 We went to Paris in November, where there are few tourists.

C **관계사의 쓰임에 주의하여 다음 문장의 뜻을 바르게 나타낸 것을 고르시오.**

1 I have many friends. One of them lives with me. He's moving away soon.

a. My friend who lives with me is moving away soon.

b. My friend, who lives with me, is moving away soon.

2 I have two jackets. My mom bought one of them for me. That one suits me best.

a. The jacket which my mom bought for me suits me best.

b. The jacket, which my mom bought for me, suits me best.

3 We went to the bank, and there I opened a savings account.

a. We went to the bank where I opened a savings account.

b. We went to the bank, where I opened a savings account.

WRITING PRACTICE

괄호 안의 말을 이용하여 영작을 완성하시오.

1 어머니가 그림을 나에게 주셨는데, 나는 그것을 내 방 벽에 걸었다. (hang)

My mother gave me a picture, ______ ______ ______ on the wall of my room.

2 그는 뉴욕에서 공부를 했는데, 거기서 그의 부인을 만났다. (wife)

He studied in New York, ______ ______ ______ ______ ______.

3 그는 내게 런던을 구경시켜 주었는데, 그것은 아주 친절한 일이었다. (very, kind)

He showed me around London, ______ ______ ______ ______ of him.

4 남편이 변호사인 Betty는 예술가이다. (husband, a lawyer)

Betty, ______ ______ ______ ______ ______, is an artist.

UNIT 47 관계사와 전치사, 복합관계사

정답 및 해설 p.14

CHECK UP 괄호 안에서 알맞은 것을 고르시오.

1 Is this the magazine for (which / that) you were looking? A-1

2 This is the girl (whom / to whom) I'm going to get married. A-1

3 This is the town (where / which) Thomas Edison was born in. A-2

4 There's plenty of food. Please eat (whoever / whatever) you want. B-1

5 I'd rather buy a luxury car, (however / whatever) expensive it may be. B-2

A 보기에서 알맞은 것을 골라 빈칸에 쓰시오.

보기 whatever whoever wherever

1 You may leave your jacket __________ you like.

2 I think it's wrong to let children do __________ they like.

3 __________ wins the tennis match will advance to the semifinals.

B 주어진 문장과 같은 뜻이 되도록 빈칸에 알맞은 복합관계사를 쓰시오.

1 No matter which of these rings you choose, I'll buy it for you.
= __________ of these rings you choose, I'll buy it for you.

2 Every time I call him, he's not in his office.
= __________ I call him, he's not in his office.

3 No matter what she puts on, she looks like a fashion model.
= __________ she puts on, she looks like a fashion model.

4 No matter how hard she studies math, she doesn't get good grades.
= __________ hard she studies math, she doesn't get good grades.

5 Anyone who sees that sad movie will cry.
= __________ sees that sad movie will cry.

C

다음 문장의 밑줄 친 부분을 고쳐 쓰시오. 틀리지 않았으면 O표 하시오.

1 This is the church in that we met last Christmas.
2 Whoever team wins this game will get to play in the World Series.
3 Anyone helps the police catch the thief will get a big reward.
4 Wherever the actor went, his fans welcomed him.
5 Yesterday I visited the San Diego Zoo, to I'd never been before.

D

괄호 안의 말을 알맞게 배열하여 문장을 완성하시오.

1 I've forgotten the name of the saleswoman (spoke, whom, I, to, on the phone).
2 You (whatever, like, post, can, you) on our website.
3 (tried, hard, however, she), she could not stop crying.
4 Four people applied for the job, (suitable, of, none, were, whom).

WRITING PRACTICE

괄호 안의 말을 이용하여 영작을 완성하시오.

1 저 여자분이 내가 네게 말했던 그 교수님이야. (about)

That woman is the professor ____________ ____________ I told you.

2 네가 무엇을 하든지 우린 너를 믿는다. (do)

We believe in you ____________ ____________ ____________.

3 내가 그녀를 볼 때마다 그녀는 선글라스를 끼고 있다. (see)

____________ ____________ ____________ ____________, she is wearing sunglasses.

4 아무리 부자라 하더라도 사람은 언제나 더 많은 것을 원한다. (rich)

____________ ____________ they ____________, people always want more.

5 우리 할아버지는 우리에게 사과 한 상자를 보내셨는데, 그중 일부는 썩어 있었다. (rotten)

My grandfather sent us a box of apples, ____________ ____________ ____________ ____________ ____________.

실전 TEST 01 Chapter 08-09

1 다음 중 어법상 맞는 것을 고르시오.

① Her innocent smile is that makes her special.
② Jessy is the person baked these cookies.
③ He was very hungry, that led him to steal the bread.
④ What was the gift which Sam gave to you?
⑤ I received a report card I was not satisfied.

[2-3] 빈칸에 공통으로 들어갈 단어를 쓰시오.

2

(A) I'll review ____________ I've just learned.
(B) ____________ makes me so angry is her dishonesty.
(C) I think ____________ you did today was really brave.

3

(A) I heard a rumor ____________ they broke up.
(B) The shoes ____________ she is wearing are new.
(C) Is there anyone ____________ can speak Spanish?

[4-5] 다음 중 밑줄 친 부분의 쓰임이 틀린 것을 고르시오.

4 ① I work with Sophie, who is my best friend.
② Whenever I see her, I can't help worrying.
③ I'll do anything that makes her happy.
④ He lost his job and friends whom he loved.
⑤ He is repairing the chair whose leg was broken.

5 ① He is the candidate who I'll vote for.
② They are friends whom can keep my secrets.
③ They got into a college which is known for having a good football team.
④ I helped a farmer whose cabin had burned down.
⑤ I'm wearing the skirt that I love the most.

6 밑줄 친 부분 중 생략할 수 없는 것을 고르시오.

① Christmas is a day when families and friends share gifts and love.
② Anyone who is interested in music is welcome to come to the concert.
③ He married the woman that I loved.
④ I talked to the people who were sitting beside me at the concert.
⑤ This is the house in which my parents live.

7 다음 밑줄 친 that 중 쓰임이 다른 하나를 고르시오.

① He runs a company that makes car parts.
② How much of the news that you hear and read do you believe?
③ This was the news that shocked the world.
④ We heard the news that the Winter Olympics will be held in our city.
⑤ This was the only news that the boy had.

[8-9] 다음 두 문장을 관계사를 이용하여 한 문장으로 바꾸시오.

8

I went to an art gallery. I saw some of Monet's paintings there.
→ I went to an art gallery, ______________ ______________________________.

9

Someone took away the pictures. They were hanging on the wall.
→ Someone took away the pictures ______________________________.

10 다음 중 어법상 맞는 것을 고르시오.

① I'm not that I used to be.
② I visited the town which my mom grew up.
③ I love hip-hop music, that most teenagers are interested in.
④ We went to a restaurant which is famous for steak.
⑤ Which road you take, you won't regret it.

11 빈칸에 알맞은 것을 고르시오.

______________ hard the test is, I'm confident I'll do well.

① How
② However
③ What
④ No matter
⑤ Whichever

12 다음 중 어법상 틀린 것을 모두 고르시오.

① You can take whatever you want.
② The girl is sitting next to me is my neighbor.
③ My team lost the game, which was disappointing.
④ Who calls, tell them I'm having a meeting.
⑤ How was the hotel where you stayed?

13 빈칸에 공통으로 들어갈 단어를 쓰시오.

(A) She was the girl ______________ used to live in Italy.
(B) ______________ could have dreamed of such a thing?
(C) Diane is the one ______________ you should rely on.

14 다음 중 어법상 틀린 것을 고르시오.

① This is the woman who I'll spend the rest of my life.
② I don't know the reason for which they love him.
③ The soldiers attacked the villagers, most of whom were innocent.
④ Wherever you go, I'll follow you.
⑤ That's how she expresses her feelings.

15 밑줄 친 부분 중 생략할 수 <u>없는</u> 것을 고르시오.

Have you been to the restaurant ① <u>which is</u> next to our school? The restaurant, ② <u>which</u> is called Joy's Pizza, is a place ③ <u>where</u> you can go for great pizza. However, the food is not the only reason ④ <u>why</u> I like to go there. I think ⑤ <u>that</u> this place makes us feel like we're eating at home.

[16-18] 빈칸에 알맞은 것을 고르시오.

16

If I ____________ in high school, I would study hard.

① am ② has ③ were
④ could ⑤ had

17

Philip got fired two years ago. If he had been a hard worker, he ____________.

① will fire ② would fire
③ would have fired ④ wouldn't be fired
⑤ wouldn't have been fired

18

I didn't have dinner. If I had eaten dinner a few hours ago, I ____________ hungry now.

① am not ② were not
③ will not be ④ would not be
⑤ wouldn't have been

19 (A), (B), (C) 각 네모 안에서 어법에 맞는 표현을 골라 짝지은 것을 고르시오.

I miss her so much. I (A) [wish / hope] she were here now. If my parents hadn't objected, I (B) [will / would] have married her. I feel sad whenever I pass by the restaurant (C) [where / which] we broke up.

	(A)		(B)		(C)
①	wish	……	will	……	where
②	wish	……	would	……	where
③	hope	……	would	……	which
④	hope	……	will	……	where
⑤	wish	……	would	……	which

20 빈칸에 들어갈 수 <u>없는</u> 것을 고르시오.

________________________, they would make a lot of money.

① If they had invested in stocks
② If they were movie stars
③ If they invent a hydrogen car
④ If they sold their house
⑤ If they had their own business

21 다음 문장을 가정법 문장으로 바르게 고친 것을 고르시오.

As the road was icy, I slipped.

① If the road were icy, I would have slipped.
② If the road weren't icy, I wouldn't slip.
③ If the road had been icy, I would have slipped.
④ If the road hadn't been icy, I won't slip.
⑤ If the road hadn't been icy, I wouldn't have slipped.

22 다음 중 어법상 틀린 것을 고르시오.

① It's cold today. I wish I wore a coat.
② It's time we went home. It's already 11.
③ Don't talk as if you were my boss.
④ A good student would not be late for school.
⑤ It had not been for the accident, he would have been a superstar.

23 밑줄 친 부분을 바르게 고친 것을 고르시오.

① I did something what I thought was right. → whom
② I interviewed Sarah, that book was my favorite. → who
③ I'm looking forward to this weekend which Sam will come back from his trip. → where
④ The package which I was waiting finally arrived. → which for
⑤ I was impressed by the way how she delivered her speech. → the way

[24-25] 다음 글을 읽고, 물음에 답하시오.

(①) There are two areas of our body that ⓐ responds to temperature. (②) One is the skin, ⓑ that senses temperature and the effect it has on our bodies. (③) The *hypothalamus controls the emotions including love, fear, anger, hatred, and sadness. (④) It also changes our body temperature ⓒ whenever it needs to adjust to the outside temperature. (⑤)

*hypothalamus 시상하부

24 글의 흐름으로 보아, 주어진 문장이 들어가기에 가장 적절한 곳을 고르시오.

The other is the hypothalamus, which is part of the brain.

25 ⓐ~ⓒ 중에서 어법상 틀린 것을 모두 찾아 바르게 고치시오.

[26-27] 다음을 읽고, 물음에 답하시오.

I had an unpleasant surprise last weekend, ________ I went to the hospital for a checkup. Unfortunately, I was diagnosed with *colon cancer. The doctor said that it could be a **familial disease. Had I known that I had a genetic risk of cancer, I ⓐ (see) my doctor more regularly. A friend of mine suggested that my diet could also be to blame. I eat lots of meat and not many vegetables. Perhaps I could have changed my diet as well, but I really don't think it would have made any difference if I ⓑ (eat) more vegetables.

*colon cancer 직장암
**familial 집안 내력인

26 위 글의 빈칸에 들어갈 말로 알맞은 것을 고르시오.

① why ② when ③ how
④ what ⑤ which

27 ⓐ와 ⓑ의 동사를 어법에 맞게 쓰시오.

UNIT 48 셀 수 있는 명사 vs. 셀 수 없는 명사

정답 및 해설 p.19

CHECK UP 괄호 안에서 알맞은 것을 고르시오.

1 These days, a lot of used (car / cars) are sold at car auctions. B-1
2 They were so poor that they couldn't even afford to buy (a food / food). C-3
3 On most flights, you can check in only two (luggages / pieces of luggage). C-4

A 보기에서 알맞은 것을 골라 빈칸에 알맞은 형태로 쓰시오.

보기 name luck fact furniture water

1 I'm just calling to wish you good ________________ with your job interview on Tuesday.
2 The Internet makes it easy to find ________________ about any subject.
3 My back started to hurt after I moved ________________ all afternoon.
4 I'm thirsty. Could I have some ________________, please?
5 Here is the annual list of the 100 most popular baby ________________ in England.

B 보기에서 알맞은 것을 골라 빈칸에 알맞은 형태로 쓰시오. (단, 한 번씩만 쓸 것)

보기 carton spoonful bottle loaf item

1 How many ________________ of sugar do you put in your coffee?
2 I usually buy two ________________ of bread every week.
3 I'll have a(n) ________________ of beer, please.
4 My son drinks as much as two ________________ of milk a day.
5 There is a(n) ________________ of news that may interest you.

C

다음 문장의 밑줄 친 부분을 고쳐 쓰시오. 틀리지 않았으면 O표 하시오.

1. I'm looking for place to buy curtains for my living room.
2. If you ask me, the biggest problem in Seoul is the traffics.
3. Liz has never scolded her son for his bad behavior.
4. We ordered two bottle of wines, which we couldn't finish.
5. The committee has finally made its decision.

D

괄호 안에서 알맞은 것을 고르시오.

1. My wife wants some (jewelry / jewelries) for her birthday. I'm thinking of buying her a pair of (earring / earrings).
2. I need to find some (information / informations) about global warming. Could you give me a bit of (an advice / advice)?
3. Because I haven't got much (moneys / money), I can't buy as many (book / books) as you.

WRITING PRACTICE

괄호 안의 말을 이용하여 영작을 완성하시오.

1. 그 가스 폭발로 아파트 건물에 약간의 피해가 갔다. (cause, some, damage)

   The gas explosion ____________ ____________ ____________ to the apartment building.

2. 소가 근처 들판에서 한가롭게 풀을 뜯고 있다. (the cattle, graze)

   ____________ ____________ ____________ ____________ peacefully in nearby fields.

3. 나는 오늘 점심으로 케이크 두 조각과 우유 한 잔을 먹었다. (piece, glass)

   I had ____________ ____________ ____________ cake and ____________ ____________ ____________ milk for lunch.

4. 경찰은 일 년 동안 그 살인 사건을 조사해오고 있다. (the police, investigate)

   ____________ ____________ ____________ ____________ ____________ the murder case for a year.

UNIT 49 명사의 전환, 명사의 수·양을 나타내는 말

정답 및 해설 p.20

CHECK UP 괄호 안에서 알맞은 것을 고르시오.

1 Emily found (hair / a hair) in her food. A
2 Isn't it about time you had your (hair / a hair) cut? A
3 Call me if you need (a few / a little) help with your homework. B-2
4 I used to know (a few / a little) Korean words, but I've forgotten them all. B-1
5 How (much / many) planets are there in our solar system? B-1

A

괄호 안에 주어진 말과 (a) few 또는 (a) little을 이용하여 빈칸을 완성하시오.

1 I finished all my Christmas shopping __________ ago. (day)
2 As few survivors from the tsunami have been found, rescuers have __________ of finding more. (hope)
3 Now that email is so common, we receive __________. (letter)
4 This soup is too thick. Try adding __________ to it. (water)
5 People are leaving my home village because there are __________. (job)
6 With __________, I will pass my driving test. (luck)

B

빈칸에 들어갈 말을 보기에서 골라 알맞은 형태로 쓰시오.

보기	water	chair	picture	information

1 You can find more __________ about the concert in this brochure.
2 There are a lot of __________, so all of us can sit down.
3 Here, drink some __________. You must be thirsty.
4 Most of the __________ on my cell phone are landscapes.

C　다음 문장에서 어법상 틀린 곳을 찾아 고치시오. 틀린 곳이 없으면 O표 하시오.

1 The printer is out of papers. Could you refill it?
2 Our daughter is learning to swim. She hasn't had much lessons yet.
3 If you're going fishing, you ought to take along some sandwiches.
4 The number of participants is higher than we expected.
5 A huge number of people in the world is starving.

D　괄호 안에서 알맞은 것을 모두 고르시오.

1 Louise will invite (a few / a little / much) friends to her birthday party.
2 He spends (many / much / a lot of) time playing mobile games.
3 My uncle earned (lots of / many / a large amount of) money on the stock market.
4 I feel exhausted. I have (few / little / much) energy.

WRITING PRACTICE

괄호 안의 말을 이용하여 영작을 완성하시오.

1 신생아 수가 줄어들고 있다. (number, babies born)

______ ______ ______ ______ ______ has been decreasing.

2 내가 좋아하는 라디오 프로그램이 거의 없어서 나는 라디오를 잘 듣지 않는다. (radio program)

I don't listen to the radio very much because there are ______ ______ ______ that I like.

3 이 거리는 교통량이 그렇게 많지 않았다. (so, traffic)

There didn't use to be ______ ______ ______ on this street.

4 장시간의 학습은 학생들이 취미를 즐길 여지를 거의 주지 않는다. (room)

Studying for long hours leaves ______ ______ for students to enjoy their hobbies.

UNIT 50 부정관사(a[an])와 정관사(the)

정답 및 해설 p.22

CHECK UP 괄호 안에서 알맞은 것을 고르시오.

1 If you're going to Busan by bus, you'd better reserve (a / the) seat now. A-1
2 I usually take my dog out for a walk twice (a / the) day. A-4
3 Last night I saw a sad film on TV. (The / A) film was about a boy with no legs. B-1
4 President Franklin Roosevelt proclaimed (a / the) third Thursday in November as Thanksgiving Day. B-4

A

빈칸에 a[an] 또는 the 중 알맞은 것을 쓰시오.

1 People often study foreign languages on __________ Internet.
2 Amelia Earhart attempted to become __________ first woman to fly around the world.
3 It took me __________ hour to finish the math test.
4 In __________ sense, I think she's right to look for another job.
5 The hotel pays the pianist $400 __________ night!
6 Which British rock group is __________ best of all time?
7 The peregrine falcon is the fastest bird in __________ sky.

B

다음 문장에서 어법상 틀린 곳을 찾아 고치시오. 틀린 곳이 없으면 O표 하시오.

1 There's nothing I enjoy more than lying in a sun.
2 A : Let's hang this painting in a living room.
B : I think it would look better in a hallway.
3 I bought some good Chilean wine for just $12 the bottle.
4 The speed limit on this road is 50 miles an hour.

C

1~5의 부정관사 a[an]와 같은 용법으로 쓰인 것을 보기에서 찾아 각각의 기호를 쓰시오.

보기
a. My dad is an accountant.
b. In a way, I agree with her.
c. A cat is more independent than a dog.
d. Our electric bill comes to roughly $40 a month.
e. Billy usually spends his weekly allowance in a day.

1 A Mr. Williams was calling for you. [ ]
2 A bird is an animal that has feathers and lays eggs. [ ]
3 There are 365 days in a year. [ ]
4 Look, this fresh fish is two dollars a pound. [ ]
5 You'd be surprised how much money I make as a taxi driver. [ ]

WRITING PRACTICE

괄호 안의 말을 이용하여 영작을 완성하시오.

1 Sullivan 부인이라는 사람이 오늘 아침에 전화해서 메시지를 남겼어. (Mrs. Sullivan)
_______ _______ _______ called this morning and left a message.

2 은퇴 후에 나는 시골에서 살고 싶다. (country)
After retirement, I would like to live _______ _______ _______.

3 나는 오늘 밤 사촌들과 영화를 보러 간다. (go, movies)
I'm _______ _______ _______ _______ with my cousins tonight.

4 나는 보통 1년에 2번 치과에 간다. (twice)
I usually go to the dentist _______ _______ _______.

5 너는 이 책을 읽어 본 적이 있니? 나는 그 작가를 정말 좋아해. (like, author)
Have you read this book? I really _______ _______ _______.

UNIT 51 주의해야 할 관사의 쓰임

정답 및 해설 p.23

CHECK UP 괄호 안에서 알맞은 것을 고르시오.

1 I like most animals, except for (snakes / the snakes) and rats! A-2

2 Most mornings I have bacon and eggs for (breakfast / the breakfast). A-6

3 It's (such a / a such) long time since I saw you last. B-1

4 You seem tired. Why don't you go to (bed / the bed)? A-4

5 (All the furniture / The all furniture) was damaged in the fire. B-2

A 보기에서 알맞은 것을 골라 빈칸에 쓰시오. (필요한 경우 the를 붙일 것)

보기 prison email school bed people

1 I found cookie crumbs on ________________ again.

2 ________________ in this picture are my classmates.

3 The parents of new students were invited to ________________ for a personal interview.

4 Please send us all the required documents by ________________.

5 The criminal was sentenced to life in ________________.

B 괄호 안의 말을 알맞게 배열하여 문장을 완성하시오.

1 It was a lovely day at the beach. We all had (such, time, great, a).

2 Emma sings beautifully. She (voice, quite, nice, has, a).

3 (papers, all, the) in the desk drawers are mine.

4 (audience, the, half) left before the end of the play.

C **다음 문장에서 어법상 틀린 곳을 찾아 고치시오. 틀린 곳이 없으면 O표 하시오.**

1 Mr. Holmes plays the basketball every Sunday.
2 Dominique bought a TV made in the United States.
3 It usually takes me 40 minutes to go to work by the car.
4 Should we go out on Friday night?
5 Everyone in my family goes to the church on Sundays.

D **다음 문장을 읽고, 반드시 필요한 경우 관사 a[an] 또는 the를 넣으시오.**

1 Connie loves playing badminton and painting pictures.
2 Socrates was Greek philosopher.
3 We went to church to deliver a box of used clothes for charity.
4 When Jon leaves school, he wants to study marketing at university.

WRITING PRACTICE

괄호 안의 말을 이용하여 영작을 완성하시오.

1 여기에서 그 역까지 택시로 얼마나 걸릴까요? (station, taxi)
How long will it take from here ______ ______ ______ ______ ______?

2 Tim은 전화를 받지 않았어. 그는 아마 여전히 자고 있을 거야. (be, bed)
Tim didn't pick up the phone. He may still ______ ______ ______.

3 우리 반의 모든 학생이 그 소식에 귀를 기울였다. (students)
______ ______ ______ in my class listened to the news.

4 네가 어젯밤에 한 것은 아주 좋은 얘기였다. (quite, good)
That was ______ ______ ______ ______ you told me last night.

5 나는 그 영화가 전혀 좋지 않았어. 줄거리가 정말 엉터리 같았어. (such, stupid, plot)
I didn't like the movie at all. It had ______ ______ ______ ______.

UNIT 52 인칭대명사, 대명사 it

정답 및 해설 p.24

CHECK UP 괄호 안에서 알맞은 것을 고르시오.

1 (I and he / He and I) had a big argument this afternoon. A-1

2 (My some friends / Some friends of mine) have their own website. A-3

3 (It / That) is cold outside. B-1

4 (It / That) is certain that he will pass the exam. B-2

A

보기에서 알맞은 말을 골라 빈칸에 쓰시오.

보기 That's it. I couldn't help it. Let's call it a day. Give it a try. Take it easy.

1 I'm so tired these days. I wish I could relax a bit and ________________.

2 ________________ for now. Thank you for helping me.

3 I haven't used this machine before, but I'll ________________.

4 A : It's getting late, and I need to get home soon.
B : Okay. ________________.

5 A : Where have you been? I've been waiting for more than an hour!
B : Sorry, but ________________. I got stuck in the rush-hour traffic.

B

다음 문장에서 어법상 틀린 곳을 찾아 고치시오. 틀린 곳이 없으면 O표 하시오.

1 I ran into Amy's a cousin the other day.

2 I and she are the same age.

3 I found amusing to see him dance.

4 A : Who's calling, please?
B : It's Tom.

5 I'm sorry I couldn't make on time.

C

1~5의 it과 같은 용법으로 쓰인 것을 보기에서 찾아 각각의 기호를 쓰시오.

보기
a. How far is it from Seoul to Busan?
b. Is it okay to call you by your first name?
c. It was in Seoul that they met and got married.
d. She thought it unfair that she had to pay for the return shipping.
e. A : Did someone call? B : It was John. He just called to say hi.

1 It is a self-portrait that the artist has been working on. [ ]
2 It is difficult for me to remember all the names on our team. [ ]
3 It is almost 400,000 kilometers from the Earth to the Moon. [ ]
4 I found it annoying that the WiFi connection was too weak. [ ]
5 A : Who's the guy in black? B : It's Manny Lewis. [ ]

WRITING PRACTICE

괄호 안의 말을 이용하여 영작을 완성하시오.

1 오늘은 어제보다 시원하다. (cooler)
________________ today than yesterday.

2 그녀의 옷 중 몇 개는 나에게도 맞다. (some, clothes, hers)
________________ fit me, too.

3 아이스하키를 하는 것은 굉장히 신이 나. 한번 해 봐! (give, try)
Playing ice hockey is quite exciting. ________________!

4 Ted가 내 생일에 선물한 것은 바로 목걸이였다. (a necklace)
It ________________ Ted gave me on my birthday.

5 영어를 할 수 있다면 스페인어를 배우는 것이 쉽다. (easy)
________________ to learn Spanish if you can speak English.

6 나는 이 서류 전부를 작성해야 된다. 이건 터무니없다. (it, ridiculous)
I have to fill out all these forms. ________________.

UNIT 53 재귀대명사(-self), 지시대명사(this, that, these, those)

정답 및 해설 p.25

CHECK UP 괄호 안에서 알맞은 것을 고르시오.

1 Tanya's in the hospital. She hurt (her / herself) while playing outside. A-1
2 Isn't it lonely living by (you / yourself)? A-3
3 How are things going (these / those) days? B-1
4 Chicago's weather is colder than (that / those) of Seoul. B-2

A

괄호 안에 주어진 대명사를 빈칸에 알맞은 형태로 쓰시오.

1 My brother blames ______________ for everything that goes wrong. (I)
2 Cathy slipped on the icy road, but luckily she didn't hurt ______________. (she)
3 Our car broke down. Do you think you can help ______________? (we)
4 Mom works late, so my brother and I cook dinner for ______________. (we)
5 A : Can I have another serving?
B : Sure. Help ______________. (you)

B

보기에서 알맞은 것을 골라 빈칸에 쓰시오.

보기 this　that　these　those

1 Chimpanzees have similar genes to ______________ of humans.
2 I'm taking a yoga class ______________ days.
3 Amy is getting married ______________ weekend.
4 ______________ who finish the test can leave early.
5 Her acting was ______________ of a professional.
6 The movie wasn't ______________ interesting. I wouldn't recommend it.

C

다음 문장의 밑줄 친 부분을 고쳐 쓰시오.

1 Stop complaining about your teacher. Put you in her shoes for a change.

2 There was no freedom in the Soviet Union in these days.

3 Today's automobiles are much safer than these of the past.

4 That who skip the class more than once will get lower grades.

D

1~3의 that과 같은 용법으로 쓰인 것을 보기에서 찾아 각각의 기호를 쓰시오.

보기
a. The number of girls in this school is twice that of boys.
b. How much is that dress in the window?
c. Why didn't you see a doctor if you were feeling that bad?

1 I prefer this novel to that one. [ ]

2 I didn't know that unemployment among young people was that serious. [ ]

3 I think your plan is much better than that of our team. [ ]

WRITING PRACTICE

보기에 주어진 말을 이용하여 영작을 완성하시오.

보기 teach / the product / angry at / different from

1 Amanda는 파워포인트 사용법을 스스로 익혔다.

Amanda ____________ ____________ how to use PowerPoint.

2 나는 같은 실수를 다시 저질러서 나 자신에게 화가 났다.

I got ____________ ____________ ____________ for making the same mistake again.

3 이 나라의 교통 법규는 한국의 것과 다르다.

The traffic laws of this country ____________ ____________ ____________ ____________ of Korea.

4 광고에서는 상품 자체보다 이미지가 더 중요하다.

In advertising, the image is more important than ____________ ____________ ____________.

UNIT 54 부정대명사 I (some, any, each, all, most, none)

정답 및 해설 p.27

CHECK UP 괄호 안에서 알맞은 것을 고르시오.

1 Would you like (any / some) toast and coffee for breakfast? A-1

2 The committee has a meeting (each / every) three weeks. B-1

3 (Each / Every) of these products has different features. B-1

4 I can't afford to see a movie. (Every / All) I have is two dollars. B-2

5 I'm afraid there are (no / none) stores open at this late hour. B-4

A

빈칸에 some 또는 any 중 알맞은 것을 쓰시오.

1 Here, have ________________ more cake and ice cream.

2 I'm so busy that I don't have ________________ time to go out with my friends.

3 There never seems to be ________________ food in the refrigerator.

4 Would you please buy ________________ fruit for dessert?

B

보기에서 알맞은 것을 골라 빈칸에 쓰시오.

보기 every each all no none

1 The singing competition takes place ____________ other year.

2 ____________ of her fingernails was a different color.

3 Mr. Clark is a mail carrier. He drives around and delivers mail ____________ day long.

4 I wanted to fly home for Christmas, but there were ____________ flights available.

5 It's autumn. ____________ the leaves have turned red and yellow.

6 Today our teacher got angry because ____________ of the students came to class on time.

C　다음 문장의 밑줄 친 부분을 고쳐 쓰시오. 틀리지 않았으면 O표 하시오.

1 Every you've done today is complain!

2 Ten friends came to my birthday party. Each of them gave me a gift.

3 Steve spent all his money foolishly, so now he has any money left.

4 The history test was hard, but I think I answered most of the questions correctly.

5 No these books belong to me. They are all Ted's.

D　두 문장이 같은 뜻이 되도록 빈칸에 알맞은 말을 쓰시오.

1 He is no longer a fan of the singer.
= He is ________________ a fan of the singer ________________.

2 There wasn't any cereal left in the grocery store.
= There was ________________ ________________ left in the grocery store.

3 You should take this medicine every four hours.
= You should take this medicine ________________ ________________ hour.

WRITING PRACTICE

괄호 안의 말을 이용하여 영작을 완성하시오.

1 각 학생은 그 질문에 다르게 대답했다. (student)
____________ ____________ has answered the question differently.

2 냉장고에는 우유가 하나도 없다. (have, milk)
We don't ____________ ____________ ____________ in the refrigerator.

3 대부분의 관광객들이 한국에 오면 서울을 방문한다. (tourist, visit)
____________ ____________ ____________ Seoul when they come to Korea.

4 그 기간에 대해서는 정보가 없습니다. (information)
____________ ____________ is available for that time period.

5 나를 진심으로 이해해주는 친구가 단 한 명도 없다. (my friends)
____________ ____________ ____________ ____________ truly understand me.

UNIT 55 부정대명사 II (one, other, another, both, either, neither, -thing)

정답 및 해설 p.28

CHECK UP 괄호 안에서 알맞은 것을 고르시오.

1 New cars are too expensive. Maybe I should buy a used (one / it). A-1

2 Some trees keep their leaves in winter, while (others / another) lose theirs. A-2

3 You look thirsty. Can I get you (another / the other) glass of lemonade? A-3

4 If (either / neither) of them don't like the house, they won't buy it. B-2

A

보기에서 알맞은 것을 골라 빈칸에 쓰시오.

보기 one other others another the other

1 I never care about what __________ think of me.

2 Pam got three gifts for her birthday. One was from her parents, __________ was from her brother, and __________ was from me.

3 Don't just follow what __________ people do. Be yourself!

4 This computer is much faster than my old __________.

B

보기에 주어진 말과 괄호 안의 부정대명사를 이용하여 문장을 완성하시오.

보기 these books days way her hands

1 I have read __________ __________ __________ __________. (neither)

2 You can go __________ __________ to get to the mall. (either)

3 The little girl was holding balloons in __________ __________ __________ __________. (both)

4 I usually relax on weekends, but this weekend I have to work __________ __________. (both)

C 다음 문장의 밑줄 친 부분을 고쳐 쓰시오. 틀리지 않았으면 O표 하시오.

1 His shoes were worn out, so I bought new one for him.
2 These pants are too big. Can I try another pair?
3 My girlfriend and I are tired. Neither of us wants to go out tonight.
4 My old school looks just like it did when I was young. Something has changed.
5 This yard looks abandoned. Anybody should cut the grass.

D 주어진 문장과 같은 뜻이 되도록 보기에서 알맞은 것을 골라 빈칸에 쓰시오.

보기 neither anything both

1 My mother likes collecting things. So does my father.
= ________ my parents like collecting things.
2 Both of them did poorly on the test.
= ________ of them did well on the test.
3 I went shopping, but I bought nothing.
= I went shopping, but I didn't buy ________.

WRITING PRACTICE

괄호 안의 말을 이용하여 영작을 완성하시오.

1 어떤 사람들은 액션 영화를 좋아하고 다른 사람들은 코미디 영화를 좋아한다. (like)
Some people ________ action movies and ________ ________ comedies.
2 David와 나는 시험에 떨어졌다. 우리 둘 다 시험에 대비하지 않았다. (neither)
David and I failed the exam. ________ ________ ________ prepared for it.
3 다행히 그 사고에서 아무도 다치지 않았다. (be injured)
Fortunately, ________ ________ ________ in the accident.
4 너는 또 다른 회의가 필요하다고 생각하니? (have, meeting)
Do you think we need to ________ ________ ________?

UNIT 56 형용사의 기본 개념 및 역할

정답 및 해설 p.29

CHECK UP 괄호 안에서 알맞은 것을 고르시오.

1 The girl sitting by herself looked (sad / sadly). A-2

2 Suzy fell (asleep / sleeping) while watching a movie. B-2

3 The injured (was / were) treated at local hospitals. C-1

4 (He was a mere child / The child was mere) when his father died. B-1

A

보기에서 알맞은 것을 골라 빈칸에 쓰시오.

보기 live alive shy ashamed elder

1 Is it right to keep __________ animals locked in cages?

2 People think she's a(n) __________ girl, but she's really not.

3 After the tsunami, no one knew whether he was dead or __________.

4 He is __________ of the terrible mistake he made.

5 My __________ brother is a pilot. He's two years older than me.

B

다음 밑줄 친 단어와 같은 뜻으로 쓰인 것을 고르시오.

1 There were many people <u>present</u> at the church luncheon.
a. I was not <u>present</u> at last week's board meeting.
b. We are extremely busy at the <u>present</u> time.

2 I'm not <u>certain</u> what will happen.
a. He is not <u>certain</u> whether he will change jobs or not.
b. There are <u>certain</u> moments we don't want to remember.

C 다음 문장에서 어법상 틀린 곳을 찾아 고치시오. 틀린 곳이 없으면 O표 하시오.

1 Since my sister and I look alike, people think we're twins.
2 Daniel's success made his father proudly.
3 It is possible that he is still live.
4 He is always eager to conquer the unknown.
5 We have important something to talk about during today's meeting.

D 빈칸에 공통으로 들어갈 형용사를 쓰시오.

1 The woman is in grief and misses her ________ husband.
2 People honored the ________ president at a memorial service.
3 We need to hurry. I don't want to be ________ for the appointment again.

WRITING PRACTICE

괄호 안의 말을 이용하여 영작을 완성하시오.

1 나는 그 위험성을 충분히 인식하고 있다. (be, aware)

I ________ well ________ ________ the danger.

2 나는 그 회의에 참석하지 않았다. (be, present)

I ________ ________ ________ at that meeting.

3 그 작은 여자아이는 개를 무서워했다. (afraid)

The little girl ________ ________ ________ dogs.

4 그들이 제안서에 새로운 어떤 것이라도 제안했나요? (offer, anything)

Did they ________ ________ ________ in their proposal?

5 부자들은 더 부유해지고 가난한 사람들은 더 가난해지고 있다. (rich, poor)

The ________ ________ getting richer, and the ________ ________ getting poorer.

UNIT 57 부사의 기본 개념 및 역할

정답 및 해설 p.30

CHECK UP 괄호 안에서 알맞은 것을 고르시오.

1 This work is dangerous. Be sure to do it very (careful / carefully). A-1
2 Bill (always rides / rides always) his bike to school. B-1
3 The milk is old. You'd better (throw away it / throw it away). B-2
4 That plane doesn't look (enough safe / safe enough) to fly in. B-3
5 I failed the exam even though I studied (hard / hardly) for it. C-1

A

다음 문장의 알맞은 곳에 enough를 넣으시오.

1 We can't eat out tonight. We don't have money.
2 The boy is old to go to elementary school.
3 I don't have time to answer all my emails.
4 You can turn off the heater now. It's warm.
5 She is quick to win the race.

B

보기에서 알맞은 것을 골라 빈칸에 쓰시오.

보기 hard hardly late lately high highly weekly

1 I haven't seen any good movies __________. Have you?
2 In my company, we have __________ meetings to plan our work.
3 Paul kicked the ball __________ in the air, over my head.
4 You have to work __________ if you want to succeed in life.
5 Due to the heavy snow, the train arrived __________.
6 I think she is a __________ gifted young pianist.
7 Bob used to be a good student, but now he __________ studies at all.

C 다음 문장에서 어법상 틀린 곳을 찾아 고치시오. 틀린 곳이 없으면 O표 하시오.

1 The national anthem usually is sung at major sports events.
2 There was lots of trash in the park but no one picked up it.
3 You are not enough tall to ride a rollercoaster.
4 Late I've been having some really strange dreams.
5 A friendly smile is one of the keys to success.

D 괄호 안의 말을 알맞게 배열하여 문장을 완성하시오.

1 (I, work, usually) on Saturdays.
2 When you leave, please (off, the, turn, radio).
3 He (costly, learned, lesson, a) when he had an accident last year.
4 The washing machine isn't working because (in, haven't, you, it, plugged).

WRITING PRACTICE

괄호 안의 말을 이용하여 영작을 완성하시오.

1 나는 그녀를 배웅하기 위해 공항으로 갔다. (see off)
I went to the airport to ______________________________.

2 그는 이 책을 이해할 수 있을 만큼 충분히 똑똑하다. (smart, enough)
He ______________________________ to understand this book.

3 Jack은 아침을 먹을 때 항상 커피를 마신다. (drink)
Jack ______________________________ when he has breakfast.

4 내 차에는 6명의 사람들이 들어갈 만한 충분한 공간이 있다. (room for)
There is ______________________________ in my car.

5 그녀는 몇 년 동안이나 내 옆집에 살고 있지만, 나는 그녀를 거의 못 본다. (hardly, see)
She has lived next door to me for years, but I __________ ever ______________.

UNIT 58 비교급·최상급의 형태, 비교 구문

정답 및 해설 p.32

CHECK UP 괄호 안에서 알맞은 것을 고르시오.

1 I think these shoes are (comfortable / more comfortable) than those ones. A-2
2 Jennifer's class is less noisy (as / than) Carol's. B-1
3 After a good sleep, I felt (better / best) than the day before. Learn More Expressions
4 Western Europe is (very / much) more developed than Eastern Europe. B-1

A

보기에서 알맞은 것을 골라 빈칸에 비교급 형태로 쓰시오.

보기				
	heavy	hard	exciting	modern
	easily	pretty	interested	

1 Tom is very diligent. He works __________ than everyone else.
2 My apartment is really old, and I want to move to a(n) __________ one.
3 With all the souvenirs, my luggage was __________ than when I started the trip.
4 Mira is __________ in reading novels than reading poetry.
5 That pink blouse looks __________ on you than the orange one.
6 Soccer is __________ than baseball.
7 You'll fall asleep __________ if you turn off the lights.

B

다음 문장에서 어법상 틀린 곳을 찾아 고치시오. 틀린 곳이 없으면 O표 하시오.

1 On the weekends, I get up late than usual.
2 It's more expensive than I thought to see a movie.
3 Generally, public schools are cheap than private ones.
4 This brand of yogurt is clearly superior than that one.
5 My new bed is even more comfortable than my old one.

C 주어진 문장과 같은 뜻이 되도록 보기에서 알맞은 것을 골라 빈칸에 쓰시오.

보기 far than more less

1 Learning Russian is much more difficult than I imagined.
= Learning Russian is __________ more difficult than I imagined.

2 This exercise is not as difficult as the last one.
= This exercise is __________ difficult __________ the last one.

3 Money is not as important as health.
= Health is __________ important __________ money.

WRITING PRACTICE

괄호 안의 말을 이용하여 영작을 완성하시오.

1 선생님께서 나보다 여기에 더 일찍 도착하셨다. (early)
My teacher got here ________ ________ ________.

2 나는 아파트에 사는 것을 좋아한다. 그것이 주택에 사는 것보다 편리하다. (convenient)
I like living in an apartment. It is ________ ________ ________ living in a house.

3 Jake는 나보다 훨씬 더 인기가 있다. (much, popular)
Jake is ________ ________ ________ than ________ ________.

4 그 사고 이후에 그는 예전보다 더 조심히 운전한다. (carefully)
After the accident, he drives ________ ________ ________ before.

5 그 게임의 새로운 버전은 이전 것보다 훨씬 더 우수하다. (far, superior)
The new version of the game is ________ ________ ________ the old one.

6 그 가구는 우리가 생각했던 것보다 더 비쌌다. (expensive, think)
The furniture was ________ ________ ________ ________ ________.

UNIT 59 여러 가지 비교 구문

정답 및 해설 p.33

CHECK UP 괄호 안에서 알맞은 것을 고르시오.

1 The more books you read, (smarter / the smarter) you will be. B
2 As you get older, the years seem to pass by (fast and fast / faster and faster). B
3 They expect us to make a decision as (soon / sooner) as possible. A
4 This is (more boring / the most boring) video game I've ever played. C-1
5 Water is eight hundred times (as dense / denser) as air. A

A 주어진 문장과 같은 뜻이 되도록 빈칸을 채우시오.

1 I couldn't stand his rude behavior any longer.
= I could ________________ stand his rude behavior.

2 It's best to pay off your debts as soon as possible.
= It's best to pay off your debts as soon as ________________.

3 The car repairs were less expensive than I expected.
= The car repairs were not ________________ I expected.

4 The new auditorium is three times as wide as the old one.
= The new auditorium is ________________ than the old one.

B 다음 문장에서 어법상 틀린 곳을 찾아 고치시오. 틀린 곳이 없으면 O표 하시오.

1 Her house is two as far away as mine.
2 Albert Einstein was one of most influential men of the 20th century.
3 The sirens got loud and loud as the fire trucks approached.
4 The more junk food I eat, the least I like it.
5 The waves at this beach are by far the best for surfing.

C 괄호 안의 단어를 비교급 또는 최상급을 이용해 바꿔 쓰시오.

1 Russia is ______________ than all the other countries in the world. (large)
2 Vatican City is ______________ country in the world. (small)
3 Baseball is one of ______________ sports in America. (popular)
4 No building in this town is ______________ this church. (old)
5 The man was ______________ person I've ever met. (famous)

D 보기에 주어진 말을 활용하여 비교 구문을 완성하시오.

보기 reliable nice many expensive

1 I like Uncle Joe. He is ______________ ______________ of my four uncles.
2 There were twice ______________ ______________ women in the auditorium ______________ men.
3 People usually think the higher the price, ______________ ______________ ______________ the product.
4 Why don't you buy a motorcycle? It is not ______________ ______________ ______________ a car.

WRITING PRACTICE

우리말과 일치하도록 괄호 안의 말을 알맞게 배열하시오.

1 너의 불어는 점점 더 나아지고 있다.
Your French (getting, better, is, and, better).

2 그 파티에는 기껏해야 열다섯 명의 사람들이 있었다.
There (not, were, than, people, fifteen, more) at the party.

3 그 목걸이는 내가 산 것 중 가장 비싼 보석이다.
The necklace is (ever, the most, piece of jewelry, I've, expensive, bought).

4 우리 반의 어떤 학생도 Stanley만큼 똑똑하지 않다.
(is, as, no student, smart, in our class, as) Stanley.

실전 TEST 02 Chapter 10-12

1 빈칸에 들어갈 말로 알맞은 것을 고르시오. (2개)

I planned Martha's birthday party with ____________.

① some of her friends
② some her friends
③ her some friends
④ some friends of her
⑤ some friends of hers

2 [보기]의 it과 쓰임이 같은 것을 고르시오.

[보기] I found it interesting to reflect on what I learned in the class.

① It's 3 o'clock in the morning.
② That's the way it goes.
③ I thought it desirable to invite him.
④ I hate the dog because it barks at me.
⑤ I'd appreciate it if you helped me out.

3 다음 중 재귀대명사를 생략할 수 있는 것을 고르시오.

① I won't forgive myself for letting her leave.
② God helps those who help themselves.
③ I found myself thinking about her.
④ Don't worry about the mess. I'll clean it up myself.
⑤ Ben told Sue not to blame herself for the accident.

4 [보기]의 that과 쓰임이 같은 것을 고르시오.

[보기] This theory is not that hard to explain.

① I didn't want to work that weekend.
② I went to Chicago with that woman.
③ That's exactly what I meant.
④ The population of China is much larger than that of Japan.
⑤ The movie I saw yesterday was not that exciting.

5 빈칸에 알맞은 부정대명사를 쓰시오.

Cloning is a controversial subject. Some people agree with it, but ____________ don't.

6 다음 중 어법상 틀린 것을 고르시오.

① The room is so clean that I can't find a single hair in it.
② I have three papers due on Friday, and the midterm exam is next Friday.
③ I walked through the woods to get the medicine for her.
④ We have spare room in our house for guests.
⑤ I don't have time to wait for you.

정답 및 해설 p.34

7 **빈칸에 공통으로 들어갈 단어를 쓰시오.**

(A) ____________ of these exercises takes one minute to do.
(B) We have two rooms, ____________ with three beds.
(C) Tom and I hardly know ____________ other.

8 **빈칸에 알맞은 것을 고르시오.**

This necklace is one of the most valuable ____________ of jewelry I own.

① slices ② pieces
③ words ④ loaves
⑤ pounds

9 **다음 중 밑줄 친 관사의 쓰임이 틀린 것을 고르시오.**

① We went to a same college.
② In a sense, both were right.
③ Deal with problems one at a time.
④ A Mr. Smith was looking for you.
⑤ It was such an easy test.

[10-11] 우리말과 일치하도록 괄호 안의 말을 활용하여 문장을 완성하시오.

10

경찰은 여자를 체포할 충분한 증거를 갖고 있지 않았다. (evidence)

→ The police didn't have ____________ to arrest the woman.

11

내 조부모님은 꽤 오래된 주택에 사신다.
(quite, house)

→ My grandparents live in ____________.

12 **다음 중 틀린 것을 바르게 고치지 못한 것을 고르시오.**

① There are two family living in the apartment. (two family → two families)
② There is man on the street. (man → men)
③ She needs some courages to enter the job market. (some courages → some courage)
④ I drank three glass of water because I was so thirsty. (three glass → three glasses)
⑤ The police was not allowed to go there. (the police was → the police were)

13 **빈칸에 들어갈 말로 알맞은 것을 고르시오. (2개)**

Let me give you ____________ advice.

① an ② some ③ many
④ sheet of ⑤ a piece of

14 다음 밑줄 친 it 중 역할이 다른 하나를 고르시오.

① It is not easy to deal with.
② It is difficult to catch a rabbit.
③ It is true that she got married to a millionaire.
④ It is a mystery where she hid the candy.
⑤ It is unknown to the public when the show starts.

15 밑줄 친 단어 뜻이 틀린 것을 고르시오.

① I still have the presents my late husband gave to me. (작고한)
② All the guests present at the party came from Canada. (현재의)
③ He is certain of what will happen in the future. (확신하는)
④ You can take a taxi right in front of the station. (바로)
⑤ Even a child knows how to deal with the problem. (심지어 ~조차도)

16 다음 중 밑줄 친 단어의 쓰임이 바른 것을 고르시오.

① She was found live.
② My brother and I look like.
③ I take care of alone babies.
④ The show after this one is main.
⑤ She fell asleep at the concert.

17 다음 대화문 중 어색한 것을 고르시오.

① A : What do you do on Sundays?
B : I often go to the movies.
② A : When do you study?
B : Usually I study at night.
③ A : Can I turn down the volume?
B : Yes, go ahead.
④ A : This is your last chance. Okay?
B : Thanks. I won't let down you.
⑤ A : Can I see the movie?
B : No. You are not old enough.

18 (A), (B), (C) 각 네모 안에서 어법에 맞는 표현을 골라 짝지은 것을 고르시오.

(A) There is a fitness center only for the [elderly / older].
(B) He is [less / worse] thoughtful than his sister.
(C) Go ahead. I'll join you [later / lately].

	(A)		(B)		(C)
①	elderly	……	less	……	later
②	elderly	……	worse	……	later
③	older	……	worse	……	lately
④	older	……	less	……	lately
⑤	elderly	……	less	……	lately

19 우리말을 영어로 바르게 옮기지 못한 것을 고르시오.

그는 반에서 가장 키가 큰 학생이다.

① He is the tallest student in the class.
② No student in the class is as tall as him.
③ No student in the class is taller than him.
④ He is taller than any other students in the class.
⑤ He is taller than all the other students in the class.

20 **우리말과 일치하도록 ⓐ, ⓑ에 알맞은 말을 쓰시오.**

> 지금 더 좋은 교육을 받으면 받을수록 미래의 네가 더 성공할 것이다.

→ ___ⓐ___ the education you get now, ___ⓑ___ you will be in the future.

21 **다음 중 틀린 것을 바르게 고치지 못한 것을 고르시오.**

① The problem was very more serious than we thought. (very → much)
② My test score is not as bad than I expected. (than → as)
③ We must collect the evidence as quick as possible. (quick → quickly)
④ This new drone flies four times faster as the previous one. (faster → fast)
⑤ Diamond is a hardest substance on earth. (a → the)

[22-23] 다음을 읽고, 물음에 답하시오.

> Probably everyone ① has seen baby animals such as kittens and puppies play. Are they just playing to have fun? The main reason is probably ② to learn some serious life skills. Adult animals, for example, need to look for food, fight, find a mate, and get along with ③ other animals of their kind. Young animals can practice these important life skills by playing. Through play, they can act as if they were hunting for ④ food, fighting and looking for a mate. They can learn how to control their movements, how to deal with ⑤ an environment around them, and how to relate with other animals in their group.

22 **①~⑤ 중에서 어법상 틀린 것을 고르시오.**

① ② ③ ④ ⑤

23 **위 글의 주제로 알맞은 것을 고르시오.**

① looking for a mate
② the survival of the fittest
③ ways to protect nature
④ young animal activities
⑤ why baby animals play

[24-25] 다음 글을 읽고, 물음에 답하시오.

> I told Dad I really wanted earrings. He looked at me for a long time. (I wonder what grown-ups think about when they stare at you like that.) Then he kind of smiled and said, "I really hope you know what you're doing. There's a chance your ear can get infected. But if it is what really want, ⓐ go for it." He said I could tell Mom so ⓑ (arrangements, make, she, all, the, could). I couldn't believe I could finally do what I wanted!

24 **ⓐ go for it의 의미를 우리말로 쓰시오.**

25 **괄호 ⓑ 안에 주어진 말을 어법과 문맥에 맞게 배열하시오.**

UNIT 60 전치사의 역할 및 위치

정답 및 해설 p.36

CHECK UP 괄호 안에서 알맞은 것을 고르시오.

1 That was a wonderful opportunity for (she / her). B
2 We are used to (get / getting) up early. B
3 We still have a lot of things to (talk / talk about). C
4 That's the man whom I bought (the car / the car from). C

A 보기에서 알맞은 전치사를 골라 빈칸에 쓰시오.

보기 for with by in on

1 I need a ladder to stand __________________.
2 Pam always finds someone to argue __________________.
3 Whom was the national anthem sung __________________?
4 Are these the keys that you were looking __________________?
5 The house looks as if it's never been lived __________________.

B 괄호 안에서 알맞은 것을 고르시오. (전치사를 쓰지 않는 경우 X)

1 I happened to meet Sean on my way (to / X) home.
2 I'm free (on / X) the fifth of December. Can we meet then?
3 He wants to have a meeting (on / X) this month if possible.
4 My uncle came to my house (on / X) last Christmas.
5 There's a farewell party (on / X) tomorrow evening.
6 We need more chairs for people to sit (on / X).

C 다음 문장에서 어법상 틀린 곳을 찾아 고치시오. 틀린 곳이 없으면 O표 하시오.

1 What is the best way to get to City Hall from here?
2 There's nothing he wouldn't do for she.

3 That's the house which Picasso grew up in.
4 Nate is a hero. He should be looked up to.
5 They're not looking forward to drive for eight hours.
6 He took the job without know how much he was going to be paid.

D **1~3의 since와 같은 용법으로 쓰인 것을 보기에서 찾아 각각의 기호를 쓰시오.**

보기 a. I haven't been home since last Thanksgiving.
b. We haven't heard from them since.
c. It's been years since I had so much fun.

1 I went there in 2004, but I haven't been back since. [ ]
2 Heavy snow has been falling since yesterday. [ ]
3 He has suffered a lot since he came here. [ ]

WRITING PRACTICE

보기에 주어진 말을 이용하여 영작을 완성하시오.

보기 good last graduation write

1 이 시는 누가 썼니?
__________ was the poem __________ __________?

2 그 시험은 6일 동안 계속되었다.
The exams __________ __________ __________ __________.

3 그녀는 졸업 이후 계속 그 회사에서 일하고 있다.
She has been working for that company __________ __________.

4 Jimmy는 아이들을 돌보는 데 뛰어나다.
Jimmy is __________ __________ __________ after the children.

UNIT 61 시간을 나타내는 전치사

정답 및 해설 p.38

CHECK UP 괄호 안에서 알맞은 것을 고르시오.

1 We moved to this neighborhood (in / at) 2015. A-1
2 I expect you back here (within / before) an hour. A-2
3 The package should arrive (by / until) early next week. A-3
4 Kofi Annan was the Secretary General of the UN (since / from) 1997 to 2006. A-4
5 Please water the plants (for / during) my absence. A-5

A

보기에서 알맞은 전치사를 골라 빈칸에 쓰시오. (단, 한 번씩만 쓸 것)

보기 during since within until by for on

1 No one has seen the child __________ last Saturday.
2 I've had this headache __________ several days.
3 No talking is allowed __________ the exam.
4 I'm afraid I won't see you again __________ next summer.
5 The flight from LA will be arriving __________ 30 minutes.
6 The concert was held __________ Thursday night.
7 Make sure that you come back here __________ 11 o'clock.

B

다음 문장에서 어법상 틀린 곳을 찾아 고치시오. 틀린 곳이 없으면 O표 하시오.

1 It rained heavily through the night.
2 We left to go fishing at 5:00 at the morning.
3 She has gone away. She'll be away by next Monday.
4 You need to decide whether to accept the job until tomorrow.
5 It will be partly sunny during the afternoon.
6 A : What time is it?
B : It's half past six.

C 두 문장의 빈칸에 공통으로 들어갈 전치사를 쓰시오.

1 a. I'll be with you ________________ a minute.
b. The annual concert is traditionally held ________________ summer.

2 a. I haven't seen Janis ________________ a while.
b. Jeff worked on the book ________________ six years before publishing it.

3 a. I'm afraid he is very busy ________________ the moment.
b. Shall we meet ________________ seven o'clock tonight?

D 괄호 안에서 알맞은 말을 골라 대화를 완성하시오.

1 A : When will they come back?
B : I think they will stay in Miami (on / for / through) August.

2 A : Did you take notes (during / until / for) the lecture?
B : Actually, no. I recorded it instead.

3 A : I can't sleep (in / at / to) night.
B : How about taking a warm bath before going to bed?

WRITING PRACTICE

보기에 주어진 전치사와 괄호 안의 말을 이용하여 영작을 완성하시오.

보기 within before since after

1 5분 안에 구급차가 도착할 거예요. (ambulance)
A(n) __________ will arrive __________ __________ __________.

2 10시 이후에 저희에게 다시 전화해 주세요. (call)
Please __________ us again __________ ten o'clock.

3 나는 지난주부터 그것에 대해 알고 있었다. (know)
I __________ __________ about it __________ __________ week.

4 나는 은행이 문을 닫기 전에 그곳을 꼭 도착해야 한다. (closing time)
I must get to the bank __________ __________ __________.

UNIT 62 장소를 나타내는 전치사 I

정답 및 해설 p.39

CHECK UP 괄호 안에서 알맞은 것을 고르시오.

1 In Sydney, the temperature almost never drops (below / under) zero. p

2 Jane sat down on the bench (between / among) Sue and Kirk. i

3 Leaping (above / over) the fence, the rabbit got into the garden and ate my plants. m

4 We drove south (toward / on) the sea. t

5 I usually wake up at six for my early morning jog (along / through) the lake. v

6 Hang this picture (on / at) the wall. e

A 다음은 Top High School 학생들이 마라톤을 할 코스를 순서대로 설명한 것이다. 그림을 보고 보기에서 알맞은 전치사를 골라 빈칸에 쓰시오. (한 번씩만 쓸 것)

보기 across under at toward along between through

The race begins **1** ________ Top High School. The runners race **2** ________ the road **3** ________ the two forests. They go **4** ________ a tunnel **5** ________ the railway. Then they run **6** ________ High Bridge and **7** ________ the tennis court. They pass the tennis court and finish in City Park.

B 괄호 안에서 알맞은 전치사를 골라 문장을 완성하시오.

1 I sat ________________ Greg and looked into his eyes. (above / from / beside)

2 The bird flew high ________________ the trees. (against / at / above)

3 Meet me at the station ________________ the clock tower. (between / under / up)

4 Tracy went ________________ the stairs and ________________ her office. (into / off / up / over)

C 보기에서 알맞은 전치사를 골라 빈칸에 쓰시오.

보기	from	on	out of	next to	off

1 My parents' apartment is ________________ the tenth floor.

2 Please keep your hands ________________ the wild flowers.

3 How long does it take to get ________________ Seoul to Tokyo?

4 We walked ________________ the house to find the street covered in snow.

5 A : Where's your bicycle?
B : It's ________________ the back door.

WRITING PRACTICE

괄호 안의 말을 이용하여 영작을 완성하시오.

1 이 도로는 그 건물들을 통과해서 공원으로 이어진다. (lead, buildings)

The road __________ __________ __________ __________ to the park.

2 Tom과 나는 그 길을 따라 나무들을 통과하여 걸었다. (walk)

Tom and I __________ __________ the path __________ the trees.

3 Owen 씨는 그의 친구들 사이에 서 있었다. (his friends)

Mr. Owen __________ __________ __________ __________.

4 계단을 내려가고 있는 저 사람 Peter 아니니? (the stairs)

Isn't that Peter __________ __________ __________ __________?

UNIT 63 장소를 나타내는 전치사 II (in, at, on의 구별)

정답 및 해설 p.40

CHECK UP 괄호 안에서 알맞은 것을 고르시오.

1 I saw Daniel while I was buying a doll (on / at) the gift shop. B
2 It was too hot (at / in) the room, so I couldn't concentrate. B
3 He got (on / in) the train without a ticket, but was caught. A
4 Do you know the man who sat (on / in) your right at the meeting? C
5 My car broke down (at / in) the middle of the bridge. C

A 보기에서 알맞은 전치사를 골라 빈칸에 쓰시오.

보기 in at on

1 I lost my bag ________________ the bus.
2 His office is ________________ the end of the hall.
3 There were a lot of people ________________ the bus stop.
4 I read about the rock festival ________________ a magazine.
5 We saw a show at the casino while we were ________________ Las Vegas.
6 Mary usually listens to the radio ________________ the car on her way to work in the morning.

B 괄호 안에 주어진 말과 전치사를 이용하여 빈칸을 완성하시오.

1 My plane lands at 12. Can you meet me ________________? (the airport)
2 I can't find my cell phone. I think I left it ________________. (the bus)
3 He was ________________ for 20 years for murder. (prison)
4 Please write your name ________________ of the document. (the bottom)
5 Kate was working ________________ during her vacation. (a farm)
6 ________________, I was always good at math and physics. (school)

C

다음 문장에서 어법상 틀린 곳을 찾아 고치시오. 틀린 곳이 없으면 O표 하시오.

1. Tom speaks Spanish well. He lived at Spain for five years.
2. There were about 4,000 people in the stadium waiting for the concert to start.
3. The doorbell is ringing. There's somebody in the door.
4. Before we plan our route, we should find our location on the map.
5. I have to stay late in work today. It's going to be a long day.

D

두 문장의 빈칸에 공통으로 들어갈 전치사를 쓰시오.

1. a. I stopped my car ________________ a red traffic light.
   b. Would you like to go to a restaurant or eat ________________ home?
2. a. My sister has a scar ________________ her left cheek.
   b. The vase standing ________________ the kitchen table was a gift from my husband.

WRITING PRACTICE

보기에 주어진 말과 전치사를 이용하여 영작을 완성하시오.

보기	country	platform	stop	hospital

1. 나는 플랫폼에서 열차를 기다리고 있다.
   I am waiting __________ __________ __________ for a train.
2. 우리 선생님은 시골에서 자랐다.
   My teacher was brought up __________ __________ __________.
3. 그녀는 병원에 얼마나 입원해 있어야 하니?
   How long does she have to __________ __________ __________ __________?
4. 당신은 다음 정거장에서 버스를 내려야 해요.
   You have to get off the bus __________ __________ __________ __________.

UNIT 64 기타 주요 전치사

정답 및 해설 p.41

CHECK UP 괄호 안에서 알맞은 것을 고르시오.

1 I've never heard (of / about) Sarah Myer. Who is she? C-2

2 This desk is made (of / from) pure oak. B-1

3 Many children in Africa are still dying (of / on) hunger. A-1

4 The only way to reach the camp is (on / by) boat. B-2

A

보기에서 알맞은 전치사를 골라 빈칸에 쓰시오.

보기 for of on from by

1 A soccer team consists ________ eleven players.

2 I felt really sorry ________ not arriving on time.

3 I don't have any cash. I'll pay for this ________ credit card.

4 I've been told to study a book ________ the history of China.

5 Let's try to think ________ something fun to do.

6 Adriana fell asleep while waiting ________ us to get here.

7 Her husband became sick ________ too much stress.

B

다음 문장을 읽고, 빈칸에 들어갈 알맞은 전치사를 고르시오.

1 Please cut this cake into four pieces ________ a knife.

a. with b. at c. through d. over

2 Did he apologize ________ what he said?

a. of b. with c. for d. about

3 Did you hear ________ the fire at the mall yesterday?

a. with b. about c. by d. on

4 The shop was closed ________ the owner's illness.

a. in b. through c. despite d. due to

C 다음 문장에서 어법상 틀린 곳을 찾아 고치시오. 틀린 곳이 없으면 O표 하시오.

1 Let's begin by do our morning exercises.

2 You can rely with me if you have any trouble.

3 The detectives prevented him from leave.

4 You can contact me anytime by email or by phone.

D 두 문장의 빈칸에 공통으로 들어갈 전치사를 쓰시오.

1 a. I need to go over your report ______________ my staff.

b. Cut along the red line ______________ a pair of scissors.

2 a. There is disagreement ______________ the definition of the problem.

b. Thick clouds hung ______________ the mountain.

3 a. The change in his status deprived him ______________ access to classified information.

b. She dreamed ______________ a future where she could spend more time drawing cartoons.

WRITING PRACTICE

괄호 안의 말을 이용하여 영작을 완성하시오.

1 이 가게에 있는 가방은 모두 가죽으로 만들어졌다. (make, leather)

All the bags in this shop ________ ________ ________ ________.

2 나는 어제 Central 공원까지 걸어서 갔다. (foot)

I went to Central Park ________ ________ yesterday.

3 나는 지난주에 내가 했던 것에 대해 생각해 봤다. (about, what)

I have ________ ________ ________ I did last week.

4 나는 더 작은 집으로 이사함으로써 용케 돈을 모을 수 있었다. (move into)

I managed to save money ________ ________ ________ a smaller house.

UNIT 65 전치사별 의미 정리

정답 및 해설 p.43

CHECK UP 괄호 안에서 알맞은 것을 고르시오.

1 We'd better hurry. We have to be there (for / by) 6 o'clock. by

2 The judge suspended my driver's license (for / in) six months. for

3 Look at that person (in / on) the funny bird costume! in

4 His injury deprived him (of / from) the chance to compete in the race. of

A 다음 밑줄 친 전치사들이 어떤 의미로 쓰였는지 바르게 연결하시오.

1 Mom took some frozen steaks <u>from</u> the freezer. •
2 Ben's face turned red <u>from</u> embarrassment. •
3 Would you please keep that baby <u>from</u> crying? •

• a. ~로 인해 (원인)
• b. ~에서, ~로부터 (출발점)
• c. ~을 못하도록 (금지)

4 He died <u>of</u> thirst in the desert. •
5 The house in the forest is made <u>of</u> wood. •
6 My grandmother loves to tell us stories <u>of</u> her childhood. •

• a. ~로 인해 (원인)
• b. ~에 대한
• c. ~으로 만든 (재료)

7 We flew one-way <u>to</u> Rome. •
8 It's a quarter <u>to</u> 3 in the afternoon. •
9 <u>To</u> my disappointment, he was not available that day. •

• a. ~전 (시각)
• b. ~하게도 (감정)
• c. ~에, ~으로 (목적지)

10 Jane had another fight <u>with</u> her boyfriend. •
11 He fell asleep <u>with</u> a book lying on his stomach. •
12 She stirred the sauce <u>with</u> a large spoon. •

• a. ~와 함께
• b. ~을 가지고 (도구)
• c. ~한 채로

B **다음 문장에서 어법상 틀린 곳을 찾아 고치시오. 틀린 곳이 없으면 O표 하시오.**

1 My dad usually gets home from work at 6 p.m.

2 He keeps fit by exercise regularly.

3 It's so nice to see you on good health.

4 In my way home I had an accident.

C **보기에서 알맞은 전치사를 골라 빈칸에 쓰시오.**

보기	on	for	to	by	at

1 ________________ my delight, she accepted my proposal.

2 Are you ________________ or against the president's proposal?

3 The kids were scolded ________________ the manager of the store.

4 Susie goes to a yoga class ________________ Wednesday afternoons.

5 My teacher was angry ________________ me for arriving late for school.

WRITING PRACTICE

보기에 주어진 전치사와 괄호 안의 말을 이용하여 영작을 완성하시오.

보기	from	on	for	beside

1 극장에 들어가자마자 나는 표를 샀다. (enter)

__________ __________ the theater, I bought tickets.

2 아이들이 싸움을 못 하도록 해주세요. (keep, fight)

Please __________ the children __________ __________.

3 나는 이 셔츠를 30달러에 샀다. (buy, shirt)

I __________ __________ __________ __________ $30.

4 우리는 서로의 옆에 앉아서 밤새 이야기했다. (sit, each other)

We __________ __________ __________ __________ and talked through the night.

UNIT 66 수의 일치, 시제의 일치

정답 및 해설 p.44

CHECK UP 괄호 안에서 알맞은 것을 고르시오.

1 Each of those boys (has / have) his own talent. A-1
2 Neither she nor I (has / have) any money. A-2
3 Doing well in sports (require / requires) lots of practice. A-5
4 Everyone said that the concert (is / was) great. B-1

A 보기에서 알맞은 것을 골라 빈칸에 쓰시오.

보기 am are is

1 Economics ____________ my least favorite subject.
2 The elderly ____________ the most likely to need medical help.
3 Not only you but also I ____________ good at swimming.
4 Twenty minutes ____________ enough time to get to the airport.
5 Most of the buildings around here ____________ more than 100 years old.
6 Making her fall in love with you ____________ not going to be easy.
7 ____________ there anyone who can explain this to me in English?
8 Two hundred dollars ____________ not a small amount of money.

B 다음 문장에서 어법상 틀린 곳을 찾아 고치시오. 틀린 곳이 없으면 O표 하시오.

1 Both my best friend and I was there.
2 Jack, as well as his friends, were late for class.
3 The number of kids affected by obesity have tripled since 1980.
4 A number of passengers have complained about the slow service at the ticket counter.
5 Most of the country enjoy pleasant weather from May to June.
6 She sang the song that he wrote for her.
7 Jack said that he eats fast food once or twice a week.
8 I know that the Joseon dynasty is founded in 1392.
9 The advantages of joining a gym is numerous.

C 주어진 문장을 시제에 유의하여 종속절로 바꾸시오.

1 "It will be cold."
→ The forecaster said that it ______________________.

2 "We are going to be late."
→ I knew that they ______________________.

3 "The Earth is round."
→ Columbus demonstrated that the Earth ______________________.

D 괄호 안에 주어진 말을 현재시제 또는 현재완료형을 이용하여 빈칸에 알맞은 형태로 쓰시오.

1 The woman in the red dress over there ______________ a lot like Liesel. (look)

2 Two bears seen roaming in the park ______________ to have escaped from a nearby zoo. (be, believed)

3 Both the conductor and the members of the orchestra ______________ about performing at Carnegie Hall. (be, excited)

4 Because of the nation's growing economy, the number of employees ______________ over the past three years. (increase)

WRITING PRACTICE

괄호 안의 말을 이용하여 영작을 완성하시오.

1 여기서 판매되는 보석 대부분은 프랑스에서 만들어졌다. (most, the jewelry)
__________ __________ __________ __________ sold here __________ made in France.

2 너뿐만 아니라 나도 이번 금요일에 뉴욕에 간다. (only, be)
__________ __________ you __________ __________ I __________ going to New York this Friday.

3 나는 어제 Dave가 경기 중에 다쳤다고 들었다. (hear, get injured)
I __________ __________ __________ __________ during a race yesterday.

4 그는 우리에게 우리가 즉시 떠나야 한다고 말했다. (must, depart)
He told us that __________ __________ __________ immediately.

UNIT 67 화법

정답 및 해설 p.46

CHECK UP 괄호 안에서 알맞은 것을 고르시오.

1 He (said / told) me that he would take me out to dinner. A-2

2 Ian said he (cleans / cleaned) his room that day. A-2

3 That guy asked me (that / whether) we had met before or not. B-1

4 The dentist advised me (don't / not to) eat too many sweets. B-2

A 다음 직접화법을 간접화법의 문장으로 고치시오. (단, 접속사 that은 생략할 것)

1 Jack said to us, "I have an idea."
→ Jack told us ______________________.

2 Yesterday Jane said to me, "I received your email last night."
→ Yesterday Jane told me ______________________.

3 A few days ago my brother said, "I have to finish my report by tomorrow."
→ A few days ago my brother said ______________________.

4 Mom said to me, "Don't be late for dinner."
→ Mom told me ______________________.

5 I asked Tom, "Did you catch any fish at the lake?"
→ I asked Tom ______________________.

6 A few weeks ago, Grace asked me, "What movie are you going to see this weekend?"
→ A few weeks ago, Grace asked me ______________________.

7 Dad said to me, "Remember to phone home."
→ Dad told me ______________________.

8 Larry said, "Let's sing a few songs."
→ Larry suggested ______________________.

B 직접화법 문장을 간접화법 문장으로 고칠 때, 밑줄 친 부분을 알맞게 고치시오.

1 "You look really pretty in your new dress."

→ Last night he told me you looked really pretty in your new dress.

2 "Come back for a second interview next Monday."

→ The interviewer told me come back for a second interview the following Monday.

3 "Hi, Mira. Did you pass the exam?"

→ Mira's friend asked her that she had passed the exam.

C 괄호 안의 말을 알맞게 배열하여 문장을 완성하시오.

1 The plumber told me (the, he, leaky, had fixed, water pipe).

2 He (that, to the city, suggested, drive, we).

3 I asked him (to the festival, was, he, coming, whether).

4 I asked her (she, had known, Matt, how long).

5 Joe wanted (if, could, to know, take, he, photos).

WRITING PRACTICE

괄호 안의 말을 이용하여 영작을 완성하시오.

1 Thomas는 나에게 실망하지 말라고 조언했다. (be disappointed)

Thomas advised me ______________________________.

2 나는 경찰에게 내 자전거를 도둑 맞았다고 말했다. (bike, be stolen)

I told the police officer that ______________________________.

3 나는 Lisa에게 그녀가 언제 선생님이 되었는지 물었다. (when, become)

I asked Lisa ______________________________.

4 Jim은 내가 전에 그 박물관에 가본 적이 있는지 물었다. (have been, the museum)

Jim asked me ______________________________ before.

UNIT 68 부정 표현, 부가의문문

정답 및 해설 p.47

CHECK UP 괄호 안에서 알맞은 것을 고르시오.

1 I (barely / don't barely) even know her. A-1

2 Some students agreed to go on a field trip to a museum. A-2
= (None / Not all) of the students agreed to go on a field trip to a museum.

3 She has a new car, (does she / doesn't she)? B

4 Be careful not to spill that drink, (shall we / will you)? B

A 주어진 문장과 같은 뜻이 되도록 보기에서 알맞은 것을 골라 빈칸에 쓰시오.

보기 without no longer nothing but neither

1 My son is only interested in playing mobile games.
= My son is interested in ________________ playing mobile games.

2 Emily doesn't work in a bank anymore.
= Emily ________________ works in a bank.

3 Every time Bill hears that joke, he laughs.
= Bill can't hear that joke ________________ laughing.

4 Sue doesn't want to go swimming, and I don't either.
= ________________ of us wants to go swimming.

B 앞 문장을 읽고, 적절한 부가의문문을 쓰시오.

1 You haven't cleaned your room yet, ________________?

2 We can go shopping this afternoon, ________________?

3 Let's eat out tonight, ________________?

4 There are two bottles of water in the refrigerator, ________________?

5 Don't behave like a child, ________________?

6 You booked the baseball tickets, ________________?

C **다음 문장의 밑줄 친 부분을 고쳐 쓰시오. 틀리지 않았으면 O표 하시오.**

1 She can't watch the movie <u>without cry</u>.
2 He has <u>few hope</u> of getting accepted to an Ivy League school.
3 You <u>cannot be too careful</u> when crossing a street.
4 Be polite, <u>shall you</u>?
5 We can't go home early, <u>can we</u>?
6 You didn't try to phone me yesterday, <u>do you</u>?

D **괄호 안의 말을 알맞게 배열하여 문장을 완성하시오.**

1 The hostages (little, have, of, chance, getting out) alive.
2 There (reason, is, any, hardly) why people should see this movie.
3 I (until, say, didn't, anything) she had finished talking.
4 Being busy (necessarily, productive, doesn't, being, mean).

WRITING PRACTICE

보기에 주어진 말과 괄호 안의 말을 이용하여 영작을 완성하시오.

보기 all few always anymore

1 그가 항상 약속을 지키는 것은 아니다. (keep)
He ________________________ his promises.

2 그녀는 더는 음악에 관심이 없다. (interested in, music)
She ________________________.

3 작년에 이곳을 방문한 관광객이 거의 없었다. (tourists)
________________________ visited this place last year.

4 나의 반 친구들 모두가 내 생일 파티에 초대된 것은 아니다. (classmate)
________________________ were invited to my birthday party.

UNIT 69 도치, 강조

정답 및 해설 p.48

CHECK UP 괄호 안에서 알맞은 것을 고르시오.

1 A : I can't believe she's getting married. A-3
B : Neither (I can / can I).

2 Hardly (I had / had I) arrived at the station when the train arrived. A-2

3 Ryan (do wants / does want) to go to college, doesn't he? B-2

4 (It / That) was at the art museum that we met for the first time. B-3

A

주어진 문장과 같은 뜻이 되도록 빈칸을 채우시오.

1 She had rarely felt so comfortable.
= Rarely ______________________ so comfortable.

2 We had hardly sat down to dinner when the phone rang.
= Hardly ______________________ when the phone rang.

3 I little knew how lucky I was to have such wonderful parents.
= Little ______________________ how lucky I was to have such wonderful parents.

4 She had no sooner stepped out of the car than the paparazzi began taking photos of her.
= No sooner ______________________ than the paparazzi began taking photos of her.

B

밑줄 친 부분을 강조하여 문장을 고쳐 쓰시오.

1 He has no interest in getting married.
→ He has no interest in getting married ______________.

2 He wrote me a letter while he was in Paris.
→ He ______________ me a letter while he was in Paris.

3 My parents sent me a card on my birthday.
→ It was ______________________________.

4 When did Amy stop by your house?
→ ______________ was it ______________________________?

C

다음 문장의 밑줄 친 부분을 고쳐 쓰시오.

1 Little I imagined that one day I would be rich.

2 Not until he got lost he decided to ask directions.

3 Who was that invented the world's first computer?

4 A : I love to go to the movies on weekends.

B : So I do.

D

괄호 안의 말을 알맞게 배열하여 문장을 완성하시오.

1 Not until I got to the store (that, I, did, remember) it was closed on Sundays.

2 Only recently (the theory, scientists, proved, have).

3 (you, in, what, world, made, the) think that she is qualified for the position?

4 Amy was lively and energetic, (most, her friends, were, as, of).

5 (have, should, you, complaints, it, about, any), return the product to the store.

WRITING PRACTICE

괄호 안의 말을 이용하여 영작을 완성하시오.

1 A : 선생님께서 하신 말씀을 못 들었어. B : 나도 그래. (neither)

A : I didn't hear what the teacher said.

B : ____________ ____________ ____________.

2 그는 그 책을 읽기 시작하자마자 잠들어 버렸다. (soon)

No ____________ ____________ ____________ started reading the book ____________ he fell asleep.

3 내게 그 편지를 보낸 사람은 바로 Sam이었다. (it, that)

____________ ____________ ____________ ____________ sent the letter to me.

4 그녀는 피하고 싶었던 바로 그 사람과 마주쳤다. (very)

She ran into ____________ ____________ ____________ she wanted to avoid.

UNIT 70 생략, 병렬관계, 삽입 및 동격, 무생물 주어 구문

정답 및 해설 p.50

CHECK UP 괄호 안에서 알맞은 것을 고르시오.

1 A : Have you seen Tom recently? A-1
B : I'm afraid (that / not).

2 The job needs to be done quickly and (efficient / efficiently). B

3 My favorite sports are swimming and (to ski / skiing). B

4 The woman was shocked by the news (of / that) his accident. C-2

A 다음 문장을 읽고, 생략할 수 있는 부분을 괄호로 묶으시오.

1 People shouldn't go outside when they are sick.

2 You can use the tools here if you need to use the tools.

3 Mike came home late, though his parents told him not to come home late.

4 He is a hard worker just as his father was a hard worker.

5 A : I think Ms. Bennett is the best English teacher we've ever had.
B : Yes, she really is the best English teacher we've ever had.

B 보기에서 알맞은 것을 골라 빈칸에 쓰시오.

보기	that	if ever	if any	I think	of

1 That's where ________ we should go tonight.

2 How many people, ________, will you hire this year?

3 I seldom, ________, go to bed before 11 p.m.

4 The idea ________ building a nuclear waste facility faced opposition.

5 The rumor ________ the actress might be replaced proved groundless.

C 다음 문장에서 어법상 틀린 곳을 찾아 고치시오. 틀린 곳이 없으면 O표 하시오.

1 The question of how to increase sales will be discussed today.

2 Her apartment was rather small but very love.

3 Tom spends his time not only studying but also to work at a part-time job.

4 Would you help him if he asked you to?

5 In this city, walking is often faster than drive.

6 We will go to dinner and then watching a movie.

D 밑줄 친 부분에 유의하여 우리말로 옮기시오.

1 A high fever prevented me from going to school.

2 Being alone usually brings me a sense of peace.

3 The poor economy has forced me to close the shop.

WRITING PRACTICE

괄호 안의 말을 이용하여 영작을 완성하시오.

1 나는 영국에서 공부하는 동안 Brian을 만났다. (while)

I met Brian ________ ________ in England.

2 Tony는 친구에게 배신당했다는 사실에 충격을 받았다. (betray)

Tony was shocked at the fact ________ ________ ________ ________ by his friend.

3 내가 기억하기로는 Megan의 생일은 7월이야. (far, remember)

Megan's birthday, ________ ________ ________ I can ________, is in July.

4 이 장치 덕택에 환자들이 움직일 수 있다. (enable, move)

This device ________ the patients ________ ________.

5 스포츠에서 가장 중요한 것은 이기는 것이 아니라 하면서 즐기는 것이다. (have fun)

The most important thing in sports is not to win but ________ ________ ________ playing.

UNIT 71 주어, 주격 보어, 목적어의 이해

정답 및 해설 p.51

CHECK UP 괄호 안에서 알맞은 것을 고르시오.

1 How did (she / her) become famous? A-1

2 I used to hate jazz music. Now I like (it / its) a lot. C-1

3 I can't believe (they said / what they said) about Peter. C-3

4 It looks rather (strange / strangely). B-1

A

다음 문장을 읽고, 밑줄 친 부분이 주어, 목적어, 보어 중 어느 것인지 쓰시오.

1 Their goal is <u>to win the World Cup</u>. [ ]

2 It requires effort <u>to achieve one's goals</u>. [ ]

3 Let me show you <u>how to use a fire extinguisher</u>. [ ]

4 <u>Being nice to others</u> will make you feel good, too. [ ]

5 My idea is <u>to create a website of my own</u>. [ ]

6 I wonder <u>whether it's going to rain tomorrow</u>. [ ]

7 I regret <u>making such a stupid decision</u>. [ ]

8 It is not fair <u>that only Jim got another chance</u>. [ ]

9 The fact is <u>that she doesn't want to get married yet</u>. [ ]

B

다음 문장에서 주어에 해당되는 부분에 밑줄을 그으시오.

1 It is essential to exercise regularly.

2 Arranging a garage sale can be a lot of work.

3 Whether you get angry or not is no concern of mine.

4 It is obvious that the meeting isn't going to start on time.

5 What we need to do is to paint the house.

C 다음 문장에서 본동사의 목적어와 보어를 찾아 밑줄을 긋고, 각각 O와 C로 표시하시오.

1 We think that you will like our proposal. [ ]

2 No one could understand what the president was saying. [ ]

3 My next plan is to travel around Europe by myself. [ ]

4 We actually asked if he needed a ride. [ ]

5 He looks angry. [ ]

D 다음 문장에서 어법상 틀린 곳을 찾아 고치시오. 틀린 곳이 없으면 O표 하시오.

1 I want talk to you about that new project.

2 James was wondering whether you'd be interested in coming to his party.

3 I suggest to contact customer service and making a complaint.

4 What you do says a lot about what you believe in.

WRITING PRACTICE

보기의 말을 이용하여 영작을 완성하시오.

보기 obvious should begin sour

1 그 음식은 신맛이 난다.

The food ______ ______.

2 그들은 무엇을 해야 하는지를 모른다.

They don't know ______ ______ ______ ______.

3 그녀가 불어를 못한다는 것은 분명하다.

______ ______ ______ ______ she doesn't speak French.

4 그 영화가 언제 시작하는지 아니?

Do you know ______ ______ ______ ______?

UNIT 72 목적격 보어의 이해

정답 및 해설 p.53

CHECK UP 괄호 안에서 알맞은 것을 고르시오.

1 Alice always keeps her desk (neat / neatly). B-1

2 Bill wants you (buy / to buy) him a sandwich. B-2

3 We watched the girls (dance / to dance) on stage. B-3

4 I'm sorry if I kept you (waiting / waited). B-4

5 I had my car (fixing / fixed) after the accident. B-5

A 다음 문장에서 목적격 보어에 해당되는 부분에 밑줄을 그으시오.

1 Her friends called her "Princess."

2 No one saw the child leave the building.

3 Let's help them unpack their bags.

4 You should have that wall painted before winter.

5 The lady over there told me to wait here until she called me.

B 주어진 문장을 목적격 보어로 사용하여 고치시오.

0 She became a super star.
→ The commercial helped her become a super star.

1 The bookshelf was poorly organized.
→ I found ______________________.

2 The light bulb was replaced.
→ I had ______________________.

3 Mom was angry.
→ My messy bedroom made ______________________.

4 The dog chased a cat up a tree.
→ We watched ______________________.

C

다음 문장에서 어법상 틀린 곳을 찾아 고치시오. 틀린 곳이 없으면 O표 하시오.

1 The boss has been keeping me very busily these days.
2 Donald got his friend to drive all the way home.
3 My mom made me to make my bed.
4 I felt my body trembling.
5 She got her coat catching in the door.

D

괄호 안에 주어진 말을 알맞은 형태로 바꾸어 빈칸에 쓰시오.

1 I won't have anything ________________ me from my goals. (deter)
2 You can't get a campfire ________________ with wet wood. (burn)
3 I want the car ________________ to its original condition. (restore)
4 He felt something ________________ up his leg. (crawl)
5 Sarah asked me ________________ what I said. (repeat)

WRITING PRACTICE

우리말과 일치하도록 괄호 안의 말을 알맞게 배열하시오.

1 선생님은 내 주제 선택이 마음에 들지 않아 내게 숙제를 다시 해 오게 했다.
(my homework, made, my teacher, redo, me) because he didn't like my choice of topic.

2 코트에 커피를 쏟아서 그것을 세탁소에 맡겨 세탁해야 한다.
I spilled coffee on my coat, so I (cleaned, to, need, it, have).

3 내 친구들이 내가 새 아파트로 이사하는 것을 도와주었다.
(move, helped, my friends, me) into my new apartment.

4 나는 네가 그 시험을 다시 보기를 원한다.
(the exam, you, to take, want, I) again.

5 내가 집에 왔을 때 나의 고양이가 소파 위에서 자고 있는 것을 봤다.
When I came home, (sleeping, I, my cat, on the sofa, saw).

UNIT 73 수식어의 이해

정답 및 해설 p.55

CHECK UP 괄호 안에서 알맞은 것을 고르시오.

1 I've never been to such (an exciting musical / a musical exciting). A-1

2 That child always does (funny something / something funny) to make me laugh. A-1

3 Is that bed (enough comfortable / comfortable enough) for you? B-1

4 Ralph is a (highly capable / capable highly) employee. B-1

5 (Obvious / Obviously), they don't want to spend too much money on this. B-1

A

다음 문장을 읽고, 굵게 쓰인 부분을 수식하는 말에 밑줄을 그으시오.

0 I'm trying to find **someone** <u>to teach me Spanish</u>.

1 I wonder what's inside **those boxes** covered with brightly colored paper.

2 **Bob's determination** to win inspires his teammates.

3 I love **that painting** hanging on the wall.

4 Do you remember **the place** where we met for the very first time?

B

다음 문장을 읽고, 굵게 쓰인 부분을 부사적으로 수식하는 말에 밑줄을 그으시오.

0 My sister sings <u>surprisingly</u> **well**.

1 Professional soccer matches are **exciting** to watch.

2 When I got up, **I cooked bacon and eggs for breakfast**.

3 Tim usually **wears glasses** to see better.

4 Not understanding the language, **I find it hard to express myself**.

5 To hear her sing, **you would think she were Beyonce**!

6 **He didn't eat anything**, though he certainly seemed hungry.

C 다음 문장의 밑줄 친 부분이 문장 내에서 하는 역할(형용사 또는 부사)을 쓰시오.

1 Being crippled, he can't walk without crutches. [ ]
2 He and I had a nice dinner and some lively conversation. [ ]
3 I couldn't call you because you forgot to give me your phone number. [ ]
4 We can go out to eat if you prefer. [ ]
5 The witnesses testifying at the court should be protected. [ ]
6 How should I study to pass the exam? [ ]
7 This is the church that we got married in. [ ]

D 괄호 안의 말을 알맞게 배열하여 문장을 완성하시오.

1 (sitting, behind me, kicking, the man, kept) my seat.
2 They gave (who, served, a huge tip, to the waiter, them).
3 These words (impossible, are, English, to translate, into).

WRITING PRACTICE

괄호 안의 말을 이용하여 영작을 완성하시오.

1 Jamie는 그의 형이 쓴 소설을 나에게 주었다. (write, by)

Jamie gave me a novel ____ ____ ____ ____.

2 Philips 씨는 내게 호의적으로 말씀하셨다. (friendly, way)

Mr. Philips spoke to me ____ a ____ ____.

3 제 차가 고장 나서 여기까지 택시로 왔어요. (because, break down)

____ ____ ____ ____ ____, I came here by taxi.

4 고를 만한 옷이 거의 없었다. (dresses, choose from)

There were few ____ ____ ____ ____.

5 교통 체증을 피하려면 우리는 더 일찍 출발했어야 했다. (avoid, heavy traffic)

We should have left earlier ____ ____ ____ ____.

UNIT 74 해석에 주의해야 할 동사

정답 및 해설 p.56

CHECK UP 괄호 안에서 알맞은 것을 고르시오.

1 Gina just informed me (of / from) the party this weekend. B

2 Do you know why she turned (off / down) my invitation? A

3 Let's replace the broken chairs (with / for) new ones. B

4 Even experts couldn't distinguish the imitation (for / from) the original ring. B

5 They ran out (of / with) money a week after they started their trip. A

A

다음 문장을 읽고, 동사에 유의하여 빈칸에 알맞은 전치사를 쓰시오.

1 She reminds me ____________ Angelina Jolie.

2 If you don't like fish, you can substitute chicken ____________ it.

3 You shouldn't put up ____________ such terrible working conditions.

4 I mistook a man in the street ____________ someone else.

5 The angry king robbed the man ____________ everything he had.

6 The police came up ____________ a plan to decrease crime rates.

B

다음 문장을 읽고, 밑줄 친 동사가 어떤 의미로 쓰였는지 해석하시오.

1 a. A firefighter saved a little girl from the fire.
b. You can save time by doing it my way.

2 a. Her performance moved the audience to tears.
b. When did you move here from New York?

3 a. He was charged with hacking into the school's computers.
b. The rental shop charged me $2 for returning DVD late.

4 a. I happened to meet my English teacher at the market today.
b. All of our products meet our customers' demand for high quality.

C

다음 문장에서 어법상 틀린 곳을 찾아 고치시오. 틀린 곳이 없으면 O표 하시오.

1 She accused us for being lazy students.
2 I was nervous when the plane took with. It was my first flight.
3 You need to work out regularly to recover from your illness.
4 We need to replace this old TV for a new one.
5 Anna made up for forgetting her friend's birthday.

D

1~3의 appreciate와 같은 뜻으로 쓰인 것을 보기에서 찾아 각각의 기호를 쓰시오.

보기
a. Van Gogh wasn't appreciated until he was dead.
b. Not everyone appreciates the danger of global warming.
c. I would appreciate it if you could give me some advice.

1 We appreciate your kind offer. [ ]
2 I appreciated the beauty of the Greek sculpture. [ ]
3 I'm not sure if the boy appreciated the seriousness of his actions. [ ]

WRITING PRACTICE

괄호 안의 말을 이용하여 영작을 완성하시오.

1 일이 내게 아주 잘 풀려 왔다. (work, well)
Things have ________ ________ ________ for me.

2 우리 소풍은 폭풍우로 취소되어야 했다. (call)
Our excursion had to ________ ________ ________ because of the storm.

3 우리에게 약간의 정보를 제공해 주실 수 있나요? (provide)
Could you please ________ ________ ________ some information?

4 그녀는 그때 그 화재를 자신의 이웃 탓으로 돌렸다. (blame)
She ________ her neighbor ________ the ________ the other day.

실전 TEST 03 Chapter 13-15

1 다음 중 어법상 맞는 것을 모두 고르시오.

① Don't look at he.
② Who do you work?
③ They shouldn't be looked down on.
④ I'll meet you on next Saturday.
⑤ Mark has been in the hospital with the flu.

2 빈칸에 공통으로 들어갈 단어를 쓰시오.

(A) I've been in Korea ______ the end of last year.
(B) I returned home and have ______ worked as a farmer.
(C) I have worked for the company ______ I was 20.

3 (A)~(D)에 들어갈 알맞은 말로 짝지은 것을 고르시오.

A: How long have you been working on the project?
B: (A) 3 years.
A: When did you start?
B: (B) my senior year.
A: (C) when do you think you'll finish it?
B: I don't know, but I'll continue to put every effort into the project (D) we get good results.

	(A)	(B)	(C)	(D)
①	For	In	Until	by
②	At	In	Through	until
③	In	During	By	within
④	For	During	By	until
⑤	At	With	Through	by

[4-6] 빈칸에 공통으로 들어갈 단어를 고르시오.

4

• My husband and I go to church ______ Sundays.
• There is a fly ______ the ceiling.
• ______ the one hand, military life is exciting, but ______ the other, it can be stressful.

① in ② on ③ at
④ up ⑤ into

5

• I have to get ______ this crisis.
• I walked ______ the park to the station.
• The baby slept ______ the night.

① along ② through ③ across
④ around ⑤ toward

6

• He didn't have any money to pay ______ the meal.
• She will be leaving ______ New York.
• ______ that reason, I can't go there.

① at ② in ③ for
④ of ⑤ with

정답 및 해설 p.57

7 **우리말과 일치하도록 괄호 안의 말을 활용하여 문장을 완성하시오.**

> 그 아파트는 방 2개와 부엌, 그리고 욕실로 이루어져 있다. (consist)

→ The apartment ____________ two bedrooms, a kitchen, and bathroom.

8 **밑줄 친 부분을 강조하여 문장을 다시 쓰시오.**

> They did not discover the mistake until much later.

→ Not ____________________
____________________.

9 **다음 문장을 간접화법으로 바꾸어 쓰시오.**

> My friend asked me, "Where did you get your shoes?"

→ My friend ____________________
____________________.

10 **다음 중 어법상 틀린 것을 고르시오.**

① People on the bus were screaming and yelling.
② The number of applicants was more than 20.
③ About half of the water has to be replaced at least once a week.
④ I hate boring subjects such as math, economic, and English.
⑤ Because of the cancer, I have to see a doctor every two weeks.

11 **다음 중 어법상 맞는 것을 고르시오.**

① He suggested that I go home.
② She advised not to drink tap water.
③ My friend asked me that I had seen the movie.
④ I said her that I would go to Australia for my honeymoon.
⑤ Yesterday I asked her when is she going to leave.

12 **다음 중 어법상 틀린 것을 고르시오.**

① I have little doubt that we will win.
② Hardly they showed their emotions.
③ He is the very last person I would trust.
④ None of us were invited to the party.
⑤ You cannot be too careful while driving.

13 **다음 대화문에서 어법상 틀린 것을 고르시오.**

① A : I don't like chicken very much.
B : Neither do I.
② A : I'd like to have some ice cream.
B : Me, too.
③ A : I had such a nice dinner.
B : So did I.
④ A : The weather might get worse.
B : I hope not.
⑤ A : I didn't go to the ceremony.
B : I didn't, neither.

14 밑줄 친 부분이 어법상 틀린 것을 고르시오.

① You didn't do it, did you?
② Let's go to the park, will you?
③ He hasn't arrived yet, has he?
④ You can trust him, can't you?
⑤ She is not telling a lie, is she?

15 우리말과 일치하도록 ⓐ, ⓑ에 알맞은 말을 [보기]에서 골라 쓰시오.

[보기] scarcely no sooner hardly as soon as than

왕자가 키스를 하자마자 그녀는 두꺼비가 되어 버렸다.
→ ___ⓐ___ had the prince kissed her, ___ⓑ___ she turned into a toad.

16 다음 밑줄 친 부분 중 형용사 역할을 하지 않는 것을 고르시오.

① Look at the baby sleeping on the couch! She is so cute.
② I picked up the bottle carried ashore from a distant land.
③ Now is the time people stand up against injustice.
④ I walked down the hallway when I heard a cry.
⑤ The room at the top of the hotel is very expensive.

17 다음 중 어법상 맞는 것으로 짝지은 것을 고르시오.

a. Get him to translate this article, will you?
b. We had our passports stealing in Vietnam.
c. The officers made me open my suitcases.
d. Could you help me moving this sofa?
e. I saw Melanie waiting for the subway.

① a, b, c ② a, c, d
③ a, c, e ④ b, c, e
⑤ b, d, e

18 (A), (B), (C)의 각 빈칸에 들어갈 알맞은 전치사나 부사를 쓰시오.

(A) Alice informed me ________ her pregnancy.
(B) They suddenly called ________ the meeting, so we had to come back later.
(C) He didn't want to run ________ of food for the party, so he had me buy more.

19 밑줄 친 부분의 역할로 바른 것을 고르시오.

① I visited a museum where I could enjoy masterpieces. (명사)
② Let me know where you'll be in London. (형용사)
③ You don't have to go all the way to the end. You can stop whenever you like. (부사)
④ Sometimes a teacher will be listened to, whereas a parent might not. (명사)
⑤ People began looking around to see where the noise was coming from. (형용사)

20 밑줄 친 단어 뜻이 틀린 것을 고르시오.

① Those who listened to him were deeply moved. (감동시키다)
② In time, you will appreciate the beauty of this language. (진가를 알다)
③ The police have charged Mr. Bell with murder. (고발하다)
④ Although I was brought up in the country, I love cities. (문제 제기하다)
⑤ Out of the original 10 applicants, two candidates meet the requirements. (충족시키다)

[21-23] 다음을 읽고, 물음에 답하시오.

One of the *chief mate's jobs ① were to write the ship's report each day, ② describing the weather, the course, and the tides. One day the mate was so drunk ___ⓐ___ he couldn't write the report; so the captain wrote it for him and included the fact ___ⓑ___ "the mate was drunk all day." The next day the mate ③ found out about it and asked the captain about the harmful statement. "It was true, ④ wasn't it?" the captain replied. The next day the captain saw the mate's daily statement in the ship's report, ⑤ which read, "Today the captain didn't get drunk."

*chief mate 일등 항해사

21 위 글의 내용과 일치하지 않는 것을 고르시오.

① 기록을 하는 것은 일등 항해사의 몫이다.
② 선장이 일등 항해사 대신 기록한 적이 있다.
③ 어느 날 일등 항해사가 술에 취했다.
④ 선장은 사실을 기술하였다.
⑤ 일등 항해사는 거짓말을 했다.

22 ①~⑤ 중에서 어법상 틀린 것을 고르시오.

① ② ③ ④ ⑤

23 위 글의 빈칸 ⓐ, ⓑ에 공통으로 들어갈 접속사를 쓰시오.

[24-25] 다음을 읽고, 물음에 답하시오.

Dad brought Mom home early ① from work, and I could tell that she had been crying. She went straight ② to her room ③ without talking to anyone. Dad said she was going to sleep ④ on a while and we should leave her alone. Then he left. I wished I knew what had happened to them. I thought that maybe They were mad ⑤ at each other and might get a divorce.

24 화자의 심정으로 가장 알맞은 것을 고르시오.

① worried
② guilty
③ grateful
④ regretful
⑤ happy

25 ①~⑤ 중에서 어법상 틀린 것을 고르시오.

① ② ③ ④ ⑤

최종 TEST 01

[1-3] 빈칸에 알맞은 것을 고르시오.

1

He burned ____________ while cooking dinner.

① he ② him ③ his
④ himself ⑤ itself

2

Her score is twice as high ____________ it was last year.

① as ② in ③ of
④ to ⑤ than

3

You should submit your report ________ next Tuesday.

① at ② by ③ until
④ since ⑤ in

[4-5] 우리말과 일치하도록 빈칸에 알맞은 말을 쓰시오.

4

나는 지난주에 내 머리를 잘랐다.

→ I got ____________ ____________ ____________ last week.

5

그 학생들 중 아무도 그 주제에 관심이 없었다.

→ ____________ ____________ ____________ ____________ were interested in the topic.

6 **다음 대화의 빈칸에 알맞은 말을 순서대로 짝지은 것을 고르시오.**

A: Can you tell me the way ____________ the national museum?
B: Sure. Go straight for two blocks and turn right. You'll find it ____________ your right.
A: How long will it take to get there?
B: ____________ ten minutes.

① to - in - About
② for - on - For
③ for - in - Through
④ to - on - About
⑤ from - on - For

[7-9] 우리말과 일치하도록 괄호 안의 말을 바르게 배열하시오.

7

당신의 물품은 당신이 주문을 하는 시각으로부터 24시간 내에 배송됩니다. (your order, you, when, place, the time)

→ Your item is shipped within 24 hours of ________________________________.

8

> 그는 자신을 믿었을 뿐만 아니라, 주위의 모든 사람을 믿었다.
> (in, did, not only, believe, he, himself)

→ ______________________________, but he also believed in everyone around him.

9

> 모든 선수들이 올림픽에 참가할 수 있는 것은 아니다.
> (all, the athletes, take part in, not, can)

→ ______________________________ the Olympics.

10 [보기]의 it과 쓰임이 같은 것을 고르시오.

[보기] I found it difficult to park the car.

① It may rain during the parade.
② You must return it within seven days.
③ I hate it when he ignores me.
④ It was in India that he started his career.
⑤ His idea made it possible to produce more cars.

[11-13] 두 문장이 같은 의미가 되도록 빈칸에 알맞은 것을 고르시오.

11

> Without the app, I couldn't have found my way around.
> → ________ ________ ________ ________ ________ ________ the app, I couldn't have found my way around.

12

> Jim is the best player in his team.
> → Jim is ________ ________ ________ ________ player in his team.

13

> My mother said to me, "Don't worry."
> → My mother told ________ ________ ________ ________.

[14-16] 우리말을 영어로 바르게 옮긴 것을 고르시오.

14 그는 병 때문에 다른 아이들과 놀지 못했다.

① His illness kept him play with other children.
② His illness kept him playing with other children.
③ His illness prevented him not playing with other children.
④ His illness prevented him from playing with other children.
⑤ His illness prevented him to play with other children.

15 그는 나에게 개를 키운 적이 있는지 물었다.

① He told me he had raised dogs.
② He said to me that I raised dogs.
③ He asked me when I raised dogs.
④ He asked me if I had raised dogs.
⑤ He asked me if he has raised dogs.

16 오늘 너희가 배운 것을 잊지 마라.

① Forget not you learned today.
② Don't forget that you learned today.
③ Don't forget it you learned today.
④ Don't forget what you learned today.
⑤ Don't forget what did you learn today.

[17-18] 밑줄 친 부분에서 어법상 틀린 것을 바르게 고치시오.

17

I had three piece of breads for breakfast.

18

The old is said to be wiser than the young.

19 다음 중 어법상 틀린 것을 고르시오.

① If I am you, I would not do that.
② Both his parents enjoy listening to music.
③ Would you like another cup of coffee?
④ Learning to ski is not as difficult as it seems.
⑤ He said that he works out at the gym every day.

20 다음 밑줄 친 부분 중 생략할 수 없는 것을 고르시오.

① Don't drive unless you have to drive.
② I knew all the people that were present.
③ She was surprised at the words that he said.
④ Clare felt sick while she was taking the exam.
⑤ He went back to the city in which he lived as a child.

21 빈칸에 들어갈 수 없는 것을 고르시오.

There was ____________ information on the Internet.

① a lot of ② a few ③ some
④ plenty of ⑤ little

[22-23] 다음 글을 읽고, 물음에 답하시오.

How did ten-year-old Dylan Ward get the title of "Britain's Kindest Kid"? After his grandfather died, Dylan wanted to do something to thank the people ⓐ that had taken care of his grandfather when he was sick. Since he had spent a lot of time painting with his grandfather, he decided to use his artistic abilities. He made over 80 paintings and sold them at his own art show. ① This raised more than £650, ② which Dylan donated to the medical charity that had helped his grandfather. The following year, Dylan's mother entered him into the "Britain's Kindest Kid" competition—a contest for 5- to 16-year-olds who have done special things to help others. When people around the country heard Dylan's story, they decided that he should win the title.

22 위 글의 ⓐ that과 쓰임이 같은 것을 고르시오.

① It was in summer that we first met.
② Chinese word order is different from that of Korean.
③ It is necessary that we take this issue seriously.
④ I didn't know that he had moved to another city.
⑤ The number of students that study abroad is increasing.

23 ① This와 ② which가 각각 가리키는 것을 본문에서 찾아 영어로 쓰시오.

[24-25] 다음 글을 읽고, 물음에 답하시오.

Do you know that our bodies have a clock ① inside them? For example, the body becomes hottest ② around 2 p.m. So that's not a good time ③ for exercising or doing physical activity, because our bodies get tired easily. Our brains become more active ④ between 6 and 8 in the morning. So studying for an hour then ⓐ (studying, as, for, is, three hours, effective, in the afternoon, as). On the other hand, our emotions are more active in the evening and ⑤ on night. So it's better to listen to our favorite songs or watch a romantic movie then. We should listen to our body clocks carefully.

24 ①~⑤ 중에서 어법상 틀린 것을 고르시오.

① ② ③ ④ ⑤

25 괄호 ⓐ 안에 주어진 말을 어법과 문맥에 맞게 배열하시오.

최종 TEST 02

[1-2] 빈칸에 알맞은 것을 고르시오.

1

Pablo talks as if he ______________ the accident, but I know that he didn't.

① witnesses ② witnessing
③ didn't witness ④ had witnessed
⑤ had not witnessed

2

I think he is the best actor ____________ has ever lived.

① who ② which ③ that
④ what ⑤ when

3 빈칸에 들어갈 말로 알맞은 것으로 짝지은 것을 고르시오.

There were a lot of people in the park; ______________ of them were jogging, ______________ walking or cycling.

① one – another ② one - some
③ some - others ④ some - another
⑤ some – the other

4 주어진 문장을 간접 화법으로 고쳐 쓰시오.

The teacher said to us, "Does anyone know the answer to the question?"

→ The teacher asked us ____________________
______________________________________.

5 다음 대화의 빈칸에 알맞은 말을 고르시오.

A: I didn't like the new *X-Men* movie very much.
B: ________________________

① So do I. ② So did I.
③ I do so. ④ Neither did I.
⑤ I did neither.

[6-7] 우리말과 일치하도록 괄호 안의 말을 바르게 배열하시오.

6

나중에서야 나는 그가 어디로 가버렸는지 알게 되었다.
(did, find out, he, where, had gone, I)

→ Only later ____________________________
______________________________________.

7

나는 오래 달릴수록 점점 편안해졌다.
(more, I, ran, comfortable, the, longer, I, got)

→ The __________________________________
______________________________________.

정답 및 해설 p.62

8 **[보기]의 a와 쓰임이 같은 것을 고르시오.**

[보기] I go to yoga classes twice a week.

① In a sense, he is very creative.
② Can you lend me a pen, please?
③ It took me an hour to get there.
④ A dog can smell ten times better than we can.
⑤ Get a medical checkup at least once a year.

9 **[보기]의 for와 쓰임이 같은 것을 고르시오.**

[보기] I have been on a business trip for a month.

① I bought some flowers for my mother.
② She boarded a flight bound for New York.
③ Are you for or against wearing school uniforms?
④ Jim slept for 14 hours without waking.
⑤ I was charged a fee for the service.

[10-12] 두 문장이 같은 의미가 되도록 빈칸에 알맞은 말을 쓰시오.

10

I regret that I didn't call you earlier.
→ I wish ________ ________ ________ ________ ________.

11

If I had known that, I would have told you.
→ Had ________ ________ ________, I would have told you.

12

Seoul is the city in which I have lived for most of my life.
→ Seoul is the city ________ ________ ________ ________ for most of my life.

13 **밑줄 친 부분을 바르게 고치지 않은 것을 고르시오.**

① She came around to my place as quickest as she could. → as quick as
② It's high time he starts acting like a grown-up. → starting
③ Darren usually stays in the bed late on weekends. → in bed
④ He warned me staying away from him. → to stay away
⑤ Because of the earthquake, about 70 percent of the houses needs major repairs. → need

14 우리말을 영어로 바르게 옮긴 것을 고르시오.

그 법은 우리에게서 선택할 자유를 빼앗는다.

① The law robs our freedom to choose of us.
② The law robs us of our freedom to choose.
③ The law robs us for our freedom to choose.
④ The law robs us with our freedom to choose.
⑤ The law robs us that our freedom to choose.

[15-16] 어법상 틀린 곳을 찾아 고치시오. (1개)

15

Jennifer said nothing, that made her father even angrier.

16

This laptop is very faster than my previous one.

17 (A), (B), (C) 각 네모 안에서 어법에 맞는 표현을 골라 짝지은 것을 고르시오.

(A) They said I could invite [whoever / whenever] I thought would enjoy the party.
(B) A number of soldiers [was / were] wounded in the battle.
(C) It was my wife [that / what] met the bank manager yesterday.

	(A)		(B)		(C)
①	whoever	……	was	……	that
②	whenever	……	was	……	what
③	whoever	……	were	……	what
④	whenever	……	were	……	that
⑤	whoever	……	were	……	that

[18-19] 다음 중 어법상 틀린 것을 고르시오.

18 ① They serve the best pizza in the city.
② Little I dreamed that he would call me.
③ The police are investigating the murder.
④ Without you, I couldn't have done anything.
⑤ Please allow me to introduce myself.

19 ① I don't believe what he said.
② He has a daughter, who is a lawyer.
③ Most of the respondents was female.
④ I don't know the reason why he left.
⑤ Please contact us as soon as possible.

[20-21] 빈칸에 공통으로 들어갈 말로 알맞은 것을 고르시오.

20
• They flew straight ________ Paris to Seoul.
• Premature babies are more likely to suffer ________ breathing difficulties.

① from ② at ③ with
④ by ⑤ above

21
• Heaven helps ________ who help themselves.
• Our prices are lower than ________ of our competitors.

① it ② he ③ that
④ those ⑤ these

[22-23] 다음 글을 읽고, 물음에 답하시오.

(A) [Since / For] most of China's history, higher class women ① were not allowed to visit doctors when they were sick. Since doctors were usually male, women of a certain class ② couldn't have their body examine. So, the Chinese made special dolls ③ modeled after the exact body of a woman, and used them (B) [for / to] medical purposes. A woman's husband would visit a doctor in her place and explain the symptoms of her sickness to the doctor ④ by pointing to the different parts of the doll. Based on this, the doctor would decide ⑤ what was wrong and provide treatment. This custom existed in China from ancient times all the way (C) [by / until] the 20th century.

22 **(A), (B), (C)의 각 네모 안에서 어법에 맞는 표현을 골라 짝지은 것을 고르시오.**

	(A)		(B)		(C)
①	Since	……	for	……	by
②	For	……	to	……	until
③	Since	……	for	……	until
④	For	……	for	……	until
⑤	For	……	to	……	by

23 **①~⑤ 중에서 어법상 틀린 것을 고르시오.**

① ② ③ ④ ⑤

[24-25] 다음 글을 읽고, 물음에 답하시오.

One day, an old man sold everything he owned and bought ① a block of gold. Then he made a hole in the ground and buried ② it there. Every day, he would go back to look at it. A farmer that worked in the area noticed the old man's visits. The farmer went to the spot and started digging until he found the block of gold, and stole ③ it. When ⓐ (empty, found, the old man, the hole) on his next visit, he became very sad and angry. A friend saw him and gave him some advice: "Take a simple stone and bury ④ it. Then imagine that the gold is still there. It will make no difference because when the gold was there, you never used ⑤ it anyway."

24 **①~⑤ 중 가리키는 대상이 다른 하나를 고르시오.**

① ② ③ ④ ⑤

25 **괄호 ⓐ 안에 주어진 말을 어법과 문맥에 맞게 배열하시오.**

MEMO

MEMO

MEMO

MEMO

지은이

NE능률 영어교육연구소

NE능률 영어교육연구소는 혁신적이며 효율적인 영어 교재를 개발하고 영어 학습의 질을 한 단계 높이고자 노력하는 NE능률의 연구조직입니다.

GRAMMAR ZONE WORKBOOK 〈기본편 2〉

펴 낸 이	주민홍
펴 낸 곳	서울특별시 마포구 월드컵북로 396(상암동) 누리꿈스퀘어 비즈니스타워 10층 (주)NE능률 (우편번호 03925)
펴 낸 날	2017년 1월 5일 개정판 제1쇄 2023년 11월 15일 제13쇄
전 화	02 2014 7114
팩 스	02 3142 0356
홈페이지	www.neungyule.com
등록번호	제 1-68호
I S B N	979-11-253-1238-3 53740
정 가	6,500원

NE 능률

고객센터

교재 내용 문의 : contact.nebooks.co.kr (별도의 가입 절차 없이 작성 가능)
제품 구매, 교환, 불량, 반품 문의 : 02-2014-7114
☎ 전화문의는 본사 업무시간 중에만 가능합니다.

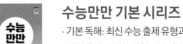

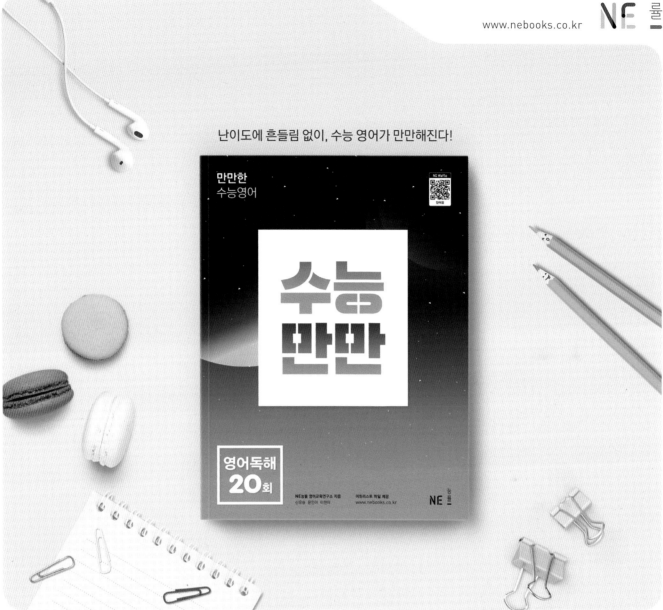